BURPEE AMERICAN GARDENING SERIES

ORCHIDS

BURPEE

AMERICAN GARDENING SERIES

ORCHIDS

Eve Kirschner Glasser

MACMILLAN • USA

This book is dedicated to my husband, Martin; my children, Elizabeth and Geoffrey; my dad, Louis Kirschner; and the memory of my mother, Frances, who gave me my first love of plants and horticulture—setting the stage for my love of nature by her example. I also dedicate this book to the many wonderful orchid growers who so graciously shared their enthusiasm and hints with me, and to my very special friends who always share their infinite knowledge, finite time, friendship, and most important, love with me, and are willing to listen to my enthusiastic rantings about how wonderful orchids are—even though until this book, they might not have totally believed it. For all of your love and encouragement, thank you!

Macmillan
A Prentice Hall Macmillan Company
15 Columbus Circle
New York, New York, 10023

Library of Congress Cataloging-in-Publication Data
Glasser, Eve.
    Orchids / Eve Glasser.
       p.   cm.—(Burpee American gardening series)
    Includes index.
    ISBN 0-671-79930-4
    1. Orchids. 2. Orchid culture. 3. Orchids—Pictorial works.
    I. Title. II. Series.
    SB409.G58 1995
    635.9'3415—dc20

    94-5205
    CIP

Designed by Levavi & Levavi

Manufactured in the United States of America

First Edition
10 9 8 7 6 5 4 3 2 1

Acknowledgments
In a general sense, I've thanked all of the orchid growers who have been a source of information and inspiration to me. More specifically I thank Lu Tempera, for often providing me with new bits of knowledge about orchids, and for making me want to know where each and every orchid comes from geographically, and the conditions it needs to grow best; to Marilyn Mirro, for taking the time to share her special growing tips with me—now there is a slight chance that my orchids will look like hers someday; to Mark Pendleton, of the Orchid Zone, for enriching this book with many of his incredible slides; to Dr. Myron Goldstein, a gentle man, a prominent physical therapist and a wonderful nature photographer, who also has shared his slides with me; and to the people at the World of Orchids in Kissimmee, Florida, who provided me with photographs and an incredible tour of their facilities. Another thank you to OFE International in Florida, who provided samples of their potting media and instruction on its use. Special thanks go to the Long Island Orchid Society and the Greater New York Orchid Society for providing help, information, plants and encouragement. A very special thank you to my two excellent editors at Macmillan, Rebecca Atwater and Rachel Simon, who offered wonderful suggestions on ways to improve the book—and who I hope, in the process, have been changed into future orchid growers. Finally, this book would not have become reality if it weren't for Suzanne Frutig Bales, author of five books in the Burpee American Gardening Series, and a special friend. She knew of my love of orchids and suggested I gather all my information, write a book and help others know the wonder of these extraordinary plants.

Photography Credits
Glasser, Eve; Goldstein, Myron; Pendleton, Mark; World of Orchids

Masdevallia Caudata 'Janet' is a wonderful orchid for the home orchid grower. Its striking appearance is enhanced by the rose-colored shimmery sepals and the yellowish orange dorsal striped with fine lines of red. This Masdevallia, when grown well, provides an exquisite specimen plant, taking little room but offering an incredible amount of beauty.

CONTENTS

INTRODUCTION

Growing orchids is one of the most exhilarating pastimes possible. Why growing orchids is oftentimes more thrilling than growing other plants is not easily explained, except for the fact that orchids have traditionally been considered "hothouse plants"—difficult to grow, impossible to bring into bloom and certainly not to be considered by anyone who didn't have access to a greenhouse. Luckily these myths are being debunked. Thousands of people the world over are growing orchids on their windowsills, under lights and in greenhouses.

Orchids are not as temperamental as one might imagine. They are rather hardy plants. In fact, they are the most plentiful plants on earth. There are more than 25,000 orchid species, and more than 50,000 varieties of the species, as well as thousands upon thousands of hybrids created by man. There are seemingly innumerable varieties of orchids available, and they are exceptionally diverse in their growing habits. With nearly a worldwide distribution (they are found in every imaginable corner of the earth), it seems fair to say that orchids are supreme in the botanical world for their incredible beauty and their great diversity.

Another unknown fact about orchids is that they are truly forgiving plants, more so than any other genera in the entire plant kingdom. They are unrivaled in adaptability when grown in captivity.

Why am I giving you all this information about orchid diversity? It's my intent to show you that, whether or not you've had success growing foliage or flowering houseplants, you can easily take part in a hobby that will add great enjoyment to your life and beauty to your home or office. In the process of growing orchids and meeting others with the same hobby, you will probably make new friends, too. Membership in local and national orchid societies has grown steadily, and there are more books written about home orchid growing now than ever before.

What is especially appealing about the art of growing orchids is that there are orchids to suit everyone. Unlike roses or African violets, which all tend to have the same shape, orchids vary widely in shape, size, color and fragrance.

There are miniature orchids, perfect for growing on a windowsill, under lights or mounted and hung in the greenhouse. The magnificent colors and patterns of these tiny orchids rival the finest art in the world. Sometimes it's even necessary to view these beautiful miniatures with a magnifying glass to appreciate the intricate work of nature's paintbrush. There are or-

A striking color contrast presents itself in this beautiful Blc. Mem. Vida Lee. A relatively easy orchid for the beginner to grow, this orchid's charm lies in its ease of flowering and the striking fuchsia of the lip and the soft lime green of the dorsal and sepals.

The strikingly beautiful Wilsonara Harlequin 'Linda' provides a very long inflorescence, totally covered with large showy flowers. The light pink lip contrasting with the vibrant red sepals and petals makes Wilsonara Harlequin 'Linda' a very special orchid.

chids, such as Standard Cymbidiums, that can grow so large they would be too cumbersome for a small greenhouse, let alone a windowsill or under lights.

Thankfully, most orchids are in the intermediate range when it comes to size, and from this group you can select from Cattleyas, Oncidiums, Paphiopedilums, Phalaenopsis, Miltonias and others. You can find almost any color of the rainbow in orchids. You could, if you wanted, grow only fragrant orchids. Your choice is limited only by the growing conditions you can provide.

Here's an example of a very well cultured Masdevallia. As seen in the photograph, there are several flowers in bloom and many buds about to open. This type of plant provides the beginning orchidist with a small growing plant that is covered with flowers for a very long time. Masdevallia Golden Tiger, typical of the genus, is a sequential bloomer.

I hope your appetite is now whetted. In this book, I have selected those orchids I believe, through my own experience, will grow and flower easily for you. You will notice in the Orchid Portraits that, although 40 different orchids are presented, most of the information concentrates on different varieties of Paphiopedilums, Phalaenopsis and Cattleyas. This is because you can easily grow a great variety of orchids from these three genera and have flowers in bloom all year long. As you become more familiar with growing orchids and achieve success with Paphiopedilums, Phalaenopsis, Cattleyas and the other orchids mentioned in the Orchid Portraits, you'll surely want to try some of the more challenging orchids. Therefore, I have listed other readily available orchids and their cultural needs in the Orchids for Enthusiasts charts.

Cymbidiums are one of the most diverse group of orchids, with flowers ranging over almost every color of the rainbow. The flowers shown here exemplify the beautiful shape of the Cymbidium and the large size of the flower. Miniature Cymbidiums are easier for the grower who doesn't have a greenhouse.

Information that will help enormously in your development as an orchid grower will come from your increasing knowledge about your own orchids. Even so, a little outside knowledge is important to start with. You must know, for example, where the orchid you want to grow comes from. If it's native to a mountainous area in South America where the temperatures are cool, where there is a constant breeze around the plants and where there is abundant rainfall, you wouldn't want to grow this plant in a hot, dry apartment. Sure, your plant might survive (orchids are very adaptable), but it wouldn't thrive.

My main objective is to provide you with the basic culture required by many different orchid genera for them to grow well. My suggestions are guidelines for orchid culture, not dogma. Growing plants well is as much an art as it is a science. Most importantly, don't be afraid to experiment with your orchids. If you admire a plant that might be described as difficult, but you think it has the most beautiful flower you've ever seen, buy it. When you own an orchid you find enthralling, the likelihood of it flowering for you is great. Growing an orchid well can be compared to developing a truly meaningful relationship. Orchids, like people, are very forgiving. The more you treasure your orchids, the more attention you'll pay to them, and the more they will bloom and prosper.

The multiflowering habit and unusual shape of Masdevallias can be clearly seen in this photo of Masdevallia Caesia.

SITES FOR ORCHID GROWING

After you decide that you'd like to try your hand at growing orchids, you face the question of where to grow your orchids for the best chance of success. Certainly any spot—except a dark basement or a dark and drafty area—will do. But most orchid growers use one or more of the following areas: a windowsill, under lights or in a greenhouse. As your love of orchids grows, you might be inclined (or forced) to use all three areas to maximize your growing space. Generally speaking, however, only one of the three is chosen.

The following scenario seems to describe the situation of most orchid growers. You receive an orchid as a gift, or purchase one, and put it on a windowsill. As it blooms and grows, you decide to acquire another orchid. Before long, the windowsills are covered with orchids. You need more room, so you investigate the possibilities of growing under lights. Finally, when you've exhausted all the room on your windowsills, under lights and in every other space in your home, the notion of a greenhouse becomes very enticing.

In this chapter, you'll learn about the advantages and requirements of these three growing situations. There are some orchids that can remain outdoors all year long in such warm areas as Hawaii, Florida and California, but this is the exception rather than the rule. Most orchid growers grow their plants on windowsills, under lights and in greenhouses.

GROWING ORCHIDS ON YOUR WINDOWSILL

Whether you live in a city apartment, a garden apartment in the suburbs or a house in a rural area, growing orchids on your windowsill can be done, and very successfully, too. The main factors to keep in mind when starting your windowsill orchid collection are the amount of light, the humidity and the space that you can provide for your plants. Your orchids will thrive if there is adequate ventilation and good air circulation.

Because there's such diversity among orchids, and because they have such varied light requirements, practically any window in your home can be converted into an orchid-growing area. Before you consider what orchids you'd like to grow, remember that the same growing conditions apply to both species and hybrid orchids. It is most important never to keep your orchids sitting in saucers of water; the roots of your orchid mustn't sit in water for any length of time or you will assuredly lose your plant. No matter how healthy the leaves, the inflorescence (flower stalk) and the flower appear to be, if the roots are mushy and waterlogged, your plant will rot. To avoid this problem, place the pot, whether clay or plastic, on a tray of pebbles or Turface (manufactured clay pebbles), so water will drain thoroughly out of the pot. Your plants

This is a beautifully grown Vanda Rothschildianum. Notice that all the leaves in the fan are healthy looking and none are missing. In vandaceous species, one of the signs of poor culture is leaves missing along the stem. This beautiful Vanda is lovingly grown by Marilyn Mirro of Long Island, New York.

There are many varieties of
Dendrobiums. Here's a beautiful
example of a Phalaenopsis-type
Dendrobium. Looking at these
flowers, you can readily see how
closely they resemble the flowers
of Phalaenopsis orchids.

This is the nobile type of
Dendrobium beautifully grown.
Well-cultured Dendrobium nobiles
produce many flowers as soon as
they reach specimen size.

will derive another benefit from sitting on top of the pebbles, and that is that the humidity in the growing area around them will increase from the moisture around the pebbles. Check daily to be sure there is enough water in the tray.

In addition to ensuring that the roots of your plant are not waterlogged, one of your main considerations is the amount of light your window will provide. In some sources, light measurements for orchids are given in terms of "footcandles"; other sources discuss light more simply, in terms of low, intermediate and high light. Plants that require high light need approximately 2,500 to 3,000 footcandles of light. Intermediate-light orchids need somewhere between 1,500 and 2,000 footcandles, and low-light orchids are those that succeed at about 1,000 footcandles.

Although the term *footcandle* may be strange to many new orchid growers, you may want to purchase a light meter when you first begin growing orchids; light meters are available through nursery suppliers, orchid suppliers, plant shops and photography stores. They accurately measure footcandles, eliminating guesswork for you. Many orchid growers insist you cannot properly grow and bloom your orchids without a light meter; others never use them. If you are unsure how much light will be provided at your window, by all means purchase a light meter. Using a light meter is the most accurate method for measuring how much light your orchids are receiving. When purchasing a footcandle-measuring light meter for orchids, try to find one that has the capability of reaching 5,000 footcandles. It's also possible to measure the amount of light your plants are receiving by using a photographic meter and converting the measurement of light into footcandles, using a table provided by the photographic meter manufacturer.

However, orchids will prosper within a wide range of footcandles, so the beginner can certainly grow orchids without needing this piece of equipment. As a matter of fact, among the many orchidists I know, very few use a light meter.

If you are willing to gauge your orchid's success by other means, such as the condition of the leaves and blooms, or general health, don't buy one. I have never used a light meter myself.

Cattleya Bob Betts is a standard-size Cattleya that produces large white flowers with yellow in the lip. Cattleya Bob Betts is a reliable bloomer and an old favorite, often used in hybridizing.

How Orchids Are Named

There is a very systematic way in which orchids are given their names:

♦ The *GENUS* name identifies the group, such as Phalaenopsis or Paphiopedilum, *to which the orchid belongs. The genus name is italicized and capitalized.*

♦ *The SPECIES identifies a naturally occurring form of the genus, such as* violacea *or* callosum. *This name appears in italics and is lower cased.*

♦ *A HYBRID name identifies the offspring of the cross-pollination of two orchids.*

♦ *The PARENTAGE refers to the pod or maternal parent crossed with the pollen or paternal parent.*

♦ *A CULTIVAR name distinguishes a special clone and always appears in single quotation marks.*

Leptotes bicolor is an ideal species, easily grown by beginners. It can be grown either mounted or in a pot.

Paphiopedilum Papa Rolf is one of the easiest of all orchids for the beginner to grow. It has beautiful soft pink and green coloration and, with the faintly veined lip, is quite a beautiful flower.

Nevertheless, if you feel you'd like to assess your light conditions, refer to the appendix on Plants and Supplies for light meter sources.

In selecting orchids to grow on your windowsill, first determine the light exposure. Is it a southern, eastern, western or northern exposure? A northern exposure provides the least light of all; a western exposure provides more, then southern, and eastern exposure, which provides the most. (Southern exposures can become very hot during the summer.) Once you determine the amount of available light, you have two choices. You can grow orchids that will bloom in the amount of light your window can provide, or you can increase or decrease the available light by adding artificial lights to your growing setup or by providing shade.

People are told to become familiar with their own bodies so that if something is wrong they'll recognize it immediately. Well, the same applies to plants. Your orchids will tell you whether they are getting enough light. If the leaves are dark green, floppy or weak, the light is too low. On the other hand, if the leaves are "washed out" and yellowish green, the light intensity is too high. Firm leaves of medium green color indicate the orchid's light requirements are being met. One pleasant aspect of orchid growing is that if your plants have weak or drooping leaves, the problem is easily rectified by placing the plants in more light. You will notice the droopy leaves straighten up in a relatively short time.

When you've determined the exposure, choose as large a window as possible for orchid growing. You'll be able to grow more plants, and they'll receive more light and even benefit from the humidity from the other plants around them. If your windowsill is not large enough to accommodate a standard-size tray, you might find someone handy to build one specifically for your conditions, or you might buy a plant table and place it in front of your window. Many successful orchid growers use this type of table setup in front of their windows, and they install lamps to increase the light intensity even more.

The most suitable trays are either Fiberglas or plastic and, obviously, they must be 100% watertight. The depth of a flat-bottomed tray should be a minimum of two inches. Fill your trays with ¼ to 1 inch of either gravel or Turface. Creative individuals have used marbles or marble chips in their trays. Remember not to fill the tray to the top with water; leave the top inch dry. You don't want your orchids sitting in water. Another type of tray is made of plastic and constructed like an egg carton; water is poured directly into the tray, and no gravel is needed as the pots sit up on dividers. There are also specially made plastic humidity trays, with a grid top that fits over a tray, which you can purchase.

You can generally find all the supplies you need at local orchid society meetings and regional orchid shows. The list of suppliers at the back of this book is another resource in your search for different types of humidity trays.

Hygrometers, like light meters, are used by some orchid growers. Generally speaking, hygrometers are invaluable to those orchid growers who have greenhouses with many hundreds of plants. However, the hygrometer is a wonderfully useful piece of equipment—for any orchid grower—as it determines the amount of humidity the plants are receiving. An inexpensive hygrometer can be found at local nurseries and through many of the suppliers listed in this book.

If you are growing your orchids in a window with a southern exposure, please take care to shade the plants with blinds, a thin curtain, a window shade or even larger plants during the hottest part of the day. Like our skin, the leaves of plants can burn quite easily because they absorb the light. You can tell if the leaves are getting too hot by touching them when the sun is shining directly on them. If they feel very hot to the touch, some protection is needed. One quick remedy is to mist the leaves with water; this cools them immediately and also provides longer-lasting protection because the moisture inside the leaf doesn't transpire as rapidly if the leaf surface is moist. Note, though; that not all orchids take kindly to misting; if your orchids are soft leaved, it's best not to mist them. Needless to say, if the leaves are exceptionally hot, you must move the plant to a different location as soon as possible.

What about temperature levels for windowsill orchids? The intermediate growers (refer to the Orchid Portraits) need

night temperatures between 55° to 62° F. Warm-growing orchids require higher night temperatures of 63° to 72° F., and cool growers thrive in temperatures ranging from 45° to 55° F.

Remember that in your home the thermostat is set for the comfort of you and your family. While it might be perfectly suitable to set the night temperature in a greenhouse to 55° F., most homeowners would balk at this notion. Most orchids grow best when the temperature is somewhat cool. Higher night temperatures tend to deplete the plant of energy that would be used to produce flowers. All orchids need a drop in night temperatures to induce flower buds. This is easier to accomplish in a greenhouse than in your home. Orchids that most need the drop in temperature at night should be placed closest to the window. But like other factors to be considered in growing orchids, don't worry if your day/night temperature fluctuations aren't that great. Remember there are other variables.

Orchids for Windowsills

Cattleyas, Cymbidiums and Ascocendas need the spot on your windowsill that receives the most light for the longest period of time. They like early morning, midday and late-afternoon sun. Oncidiums and Dendrobiums also need good light. Vandas and Ascocendas thrive in high light and will tolerate great amounts of sunlight. However, because Vandas require a great deal of growing space, high humidity and exceptional air circulation to bloom well, they are for the most part not suitable for windowsill growing. Ascocendas, on the other hand, can be wonderful plants for a southern exposure if placed in hanging wooden baskets or mounted with hangers attached. They enjoy even more light when hung near the top of your window frame. Paphiopedilums and Phalaenopsis need low light, either shielded from the noon-day sun or placed in the shadow of larger, more sun-tolerant plants. Many Paphiopedilums and Phalaenopsis will even bloom in areas of your home that don't get full sun, but only filtered light. If you have a very cool windowsill, you will do well with Masdevallias, some Draculas, and the cool-growing Colombian Miltonias.

GROWING ORCHIDS UNDER LIGHTS

Although some people consider a greenhouse to be the ideal situation for growing orchids, many others grow orchids under lights; they do a marvelous job, showing their orchids at local orchid society meetings as well as at American Orchid Society events. What's so advantageous about growing orchids under lights? For one thing, you can put an otherwise

These Oncidium flowers display soft shades of pink, bright orange and a spotted lip. Although these plants have relatively small flowers, they are so floriferous that they make a wonderful display.

unused area—an attic, basement or other empty room—to good use. Simply set up a light table, and you have an ideal place for growing orchids. Not every home has large, spacious windows for growing orchids, but most apartments and houses have a spot in which to set up a light table.

Another advantage to growing orchids under lights is that you control the environment. In a greenhouse, the hours of sunshine are controlled by natural conditions. For instance, if it rains for a week, the amount of sunlight for your greenhouse orchids is nil. However, if you grow orchids under lights, you control the light source, so each day your orchids receive the maximum amount of light your setup can provide. By connecting your lights to a timer, you can program the hours of "daylight" your orchids receive to mimic nature, without having to adjust the lights constantly yourself. For example, in spring and summer, you increase the number of hours your orchids receive light; as you approach fall, gradually decrease the light hours until winter when the light levels are the lowest. Without a timer, you will have to remember when to turn the lights on and off yourself.

These are my orchids growing on a four-tiered light table in my basement. As you can see, many plants can be accommodated on each shelf.

The mechanics of growing orchids under lights is limited only by your imagination, your handiness and the amount of money you have to spend on equipment. Shelves can be built to accommodate fluorescent lights. Large halogen bulbs can be hung over your orchids. If you are not familiar with electrical work, you may want to call an electrician to install the lighting once the shelves are constructed. Use light fixtures with reflectors, if possible, to increase the light.

Easiest and most expeditious are ready-made two-, three- or four-tiered light tables, with space for four or eight 40-watt bulbs apiece. These tables often come with wheels so that they can be moved from one area of your home to another. Although the cost of ready-made light tables is fairly high (from $300 to $600, without the light bulbs), these are sturdy pieces of equipment which, given good care, will last a lifetime. All you will have to replace are the light bulbs every year or two.

When choosing lights for your light tables, remember that the red and blue portions of the light spectrum are the ones most needed by plants for photosynthesis. You can satisfy their light requirements with fluorescent light. However, because the red portion of the spectrum is the one that encourages flowering and greater growth, you should try to combine incandescent and fluorescent lights, as incandescent lights provide more red light. If only incandescent lights were used, they would have to be placed so close to the plants that they would burn them. A number of high-intensity lights designed for growing plants are available through orchid supply houses, greenhouse suppliers and most large commercial nurseries. Some of the more

Renanthera monachica *when in bloom is truly a magnificent sight. The flowers, although relatively small, are brilliantly colored and nicely arranged on the inflorescence.*

During the summer months, all of my orchids vacation outside where they benefit greatly from the summer winds, good air circulation and light.

well-known plant lights are Tru-Lux, Vita Light and Power Twist.

The most popular light table setup uses four tube-shaped, 40-watt bulbs per shelf. For this or any other light table, place those orchids that require the most light closest to the bulbs. Many beginners are afraid of placing their plants too close to the light, and because of this they can't get their plants to bloom. A few inches closer to the light will make the difference between a nonblooming and a flowering orchid. The light is strongest at the center of the bulb, so place your Cattleyas, Oncidiums, Dendrobiums and Epidendrums about 3 to 3½ inches from the light and around the center of the bulb. Place Phalaenopsis, Paphiopedilums and other orchids requiring less light about 12 inches from the light and toward the ends of the bulb. Adjusting the light level is rather easy. If you have a prefabricated light table, it probably is fitted with chains on either end of each shelf that enable you to raise or lower the bulbs. In the case of a homemade setup, you can bring your high light–loving orchids closer to the light by setting them on inverted pots.

Ensure maximum light by cleaning and regularly replacing the bulbs. Manufacturers indicate the life expectancy for their bulbs on the package, but don't wait for this date. As the bulbs near their expiration, the light they provide diminishes. Without sufficient lights your plants will suffer. You might want to record the date you put

a lamp into your fixture to keep track of its replacement.

How many hours of artificial light do orchids need? Opinions vary, but the general consensus seems to be 14 to 16 hours of light each day. You can make seasonal adjustments to the hours in your light setup, with longer exposure in spring and summer, briefer exposure in fall and even less in winter. I like to try to imitate the hours

Construction of the plant stands for summer use is simple but practical. As you can see, cinder blocks are topped with wooden boards. Trays are placed on the boards, and the orchids are set inside the trays and watered on a daily basis throughout the summer (when the day is sunny and warm). When the temperature soars, watering is done twice a day.

of light that would naturally be available, and, of course, it is somewhat more economical to provide less light during the season of shorter days.

Again, as with your watering habits, observe your orchids. If they don't seem to set bud or flower for you, try moving them closer to the light. If the leaves are dark green, give the plants more light. Conversely, if the leaves look desiccated and very pale, move them away from the lights or decrease the number of daylight hours. Be patient if your plants don't seem to burst into bloom when first placed on your light table. They need time to adjust to their new situation. Many established orchid grow-ers have lost plants when moving them to new headquarters, so don't be upset. If you tend to your plants regularly and read their signals, they will be thriving and blooming under lights in no time.

Orchids grown under lights need basically the same conditions as those grown on a win-dowsill or in a greenhouse. They need good air circulation, which you can provide with oscillating floor fans, and considerable hu-midity, which can be promoted by misting, by grouping your or-chids together and by placing the orchid pots on pebbles or Turface standing in water, as ex-plained previously. Remember, try not to crowd your plants.

Give them adequate space for good air circulation. Crowded conditions invite disease and pest problems. As in nature, or-chids growing under lights need a drop in temperature in the eve-ning to set buds. Try to decrease the night temperature in your growing area by 10° to 15° F. This can be accomplished sim-ply by opening a few windows. Do avoid a cold draft directly on the plants, though.

Prior to adding a newly ac-quired orchid to your collection, isolate it for a few days to ensure there are no pests or viruses present. This is true for plants in a greenhouse, on a windowsill or under lights.

GROWING ORCHIDS IN A GREENHOUSE

If you are just beginning to grow orchids, or have just received your first orchid plant, you prob-ably can't envision having enough orchids to warrant build-ing a greenhouse. But the time may come when you have cause to rethink this issue. Orchid growing, as many hobbyists have learned, is addictive. After you've successfully brought your first orchid plant to bloom, you'll try your hand at another, and another and another. And as you enjoy your success, you might even consider joining an orchid society in your area. This is something I strongly recom-mend. Your local orchid society is where you'll learn about the various types of orchids; pick up hints from expert growers on how to grow them; get wonderful buys on orchid plants society members are selling or dividing from their own collections; and learn how to prepare your plants for the show table. Believe it or not, one day you may bring your own orchids in for judging, and they may receive an award for outstanding culture, flower qual-ity or rarity.

No, you don't need a green-house to grow orchids. However, the variety and size of the orchid plants you can accommodate is much greater if you have a greenhouse. In addition to this, greenhouses provide lengthy pe-riods of daylight and cool nights. When many plants are grouped together, as in a greenhouse, hu-midity naturally increases; wa-tering is easier, too, because you don't have to worry about where the excess water will go, unlike watering in a basement or on a windowsill.

A greenhouse may be a glassed-in enclosure built around a win-dow (what some manufacturers refer to as a "greenhouse win-dow"), a garden room, a lean-to structure adjacent to the house

Special Orchid Growing Tips

♦ *Try not to crowd your plants; they need good circulation to survive.*

♦ *Prior to adding a newly acquired orchid to your collection, isolate it for a few days to ensure there are no pests or viruses present.*

♦ *Before you cut off a part of your orchid using a knife or scissors, make sure you sterilize the knife or scissors in a flame. That way, if any disease is present, it won't be transmitted to another orchid.*

♦ *When in doubt about watering, don't. More orchids are killed by overwatering than by any other cause.*

Here are different varieties of Vandas and Ascocendas blooming in baskets at a greenhouse in Florida. Notice that the Vandas are grown in baskets, high up in the greenhouse, with the roots growing unfettered.

or garage, or a free-standing structure. Obviously, the greater the available space for a free-standing greenhouse, the larger the greenhouse can be. If you want to build a free-standing greenhouse on your property, plan for the largest size you can accommodate. You might think to yourself, "I'll never be able to fill a greenhouse this large with my collection." But think again. Every orchid grower I know shares the same desire: "If only I had a larger greenhouse." Regardless of the size, there's never enough room for all the plants you want.

Numerous factors should be taken into consideration when growing orchids in a greenhouse: heat, humidity, light, cooling and ventilation, and watering. The balance of these climatic factors will determine which orchids grow best for you. Attached greenhouses are relatively inexpensive to build and have the advantage that water and electricity can be brought from the house into the greenhouse relatively easily. Free-standing greenhouses usually receive the greatest amount of light, as all sides of the structure are exposed, but they are

the most expensive option. Whatever the greenhouse structure you choose, it should be built where it will receive maximum sun during the day. For this reason, a southern or eastern exposure is best. You cannot increase the amount of outdoor light (without adding artificial light), but you can decrease the amount of sun by installing shades or painting the panes with whitewash.

If you join the American Orchid Society—and I cannot stress strongly enough how important this is to all orchid growers, beginners in particular—you will receive a monthly bulletin in which many manufacturers advertise greenhouses of all descriptions, both prefabricated and individually constructed. You'll need benches for your plants, and these, too, can be ordered from various suppliers, or you can build your own from cinderblocks, redwood or galvanized iron mesh.

Heat

Orchids don't survive very cold temperatures. If you live in an area where the night temperatures fall below 45° F., your greenhouse will have to be heated. There are numerous ways to provide warmth, and contacting greenhouse manufacturers and fellow orchid growers will provide you with good sources of information. In my greenhouse, I have installed baseboard heating, which is connected to the heating unit in my home. Baseboard heating is reliable, the thermostat is easily controlled, and installation is relatively easy. If your house is heated by hot water or steam, this could be brought into your greenhouse as well. Other heating choices include gas, oil or electric free-standing heaters, and gas-fired hot water systems. Whatever system you choose, it is extremely important to see that your heating system always functions as it should. An entire greenhouse filled with valuable orchids could be lost through a heat failure. Install a minimum/maximum thermometer inside your greenhouse for registering day and evening temperatures. It will alert you to inappropriate temperatures, so you can take action. These thermometers can be obtained from greenhouse suppliers and hardware stores.

Humidity

Orchids need humidity to thrive. However, too much humidity in a greenhouse must be avoided because excessive moisture combined with cloudy, gray days provides ideal conditions for diseases. Humidity for your greenhouse should be between 50% and 60%. There are many types of automatic humidifiers available, some of which work in conjunction with cooling or ventilation systems, and greenhouse suppliers are a good source. Orchid growers increase humidity in their greenhouses with fan and pad humidifiers as well as aerosol humidifiers. A hygrometer will give you an adequate reading of the humidity in your greenhouse, so you can regulate the conditions for best results.

Light

Site your greenhouse on your property where it will receive the maximum amount of light, ideally from early morning to late afternoon. Not only will this reduce your heating costs but it will also increase your flowering production. Although good light is a necessity for most orchids, too much light is to be avoided because it burns the leaves, causing the orchids to become desiccated. All glass greenhouses require some type of shading in the latter days of spring and during summer. This shading can be provided by painting the greenhouse panes with shading compounds (whitewash), covering them with shadecloth or installing electric rolling blinds over the greenhouse panels—a more expensive solution. Here again, greenhouse suppliers and many commercial nurseries are a good source for these products.

Cooling and Ventilation

As a rule, orchids growing in the wild enjoy fresh air and good circulation from the breezes that blow around them. In your greenhouse, you will need to approximate the same type of circulation, avoiding the problem of stagnant air around your plants. One of the easiest methods is to set up several fans, preferably the oscillating type, throughout the greenhouse. The fans will keep the air moving and thus help prevent the transmission of diseases.

A simple way to ensure good ventilation is by purchasing a greenhouse with vents along the top that can be opened, manually or automatically (if you want to spend the additional money) when the heat in the greenhouse exceeds a desired temperature. (During the hot, summer months, ventilation is especially important.) Some smaller green-

A profusion of orchids in all colors, sizes and shapes greets the visitor to "A World of Orchids," a wonderful educational and aesthetic facility in Kissimee, Florida.

houses have one large vent on the top of the greenhouse, rather than several small ones. Many of the newer greenhouses also have bottom vents for additional air movement.

Placing your orchids on benches made from slats will also encourage good air circulation around your plants. Benches are a very important consideration for any greenhouse. They may be flat or stepped, so that the plants sit above one another in rows. With stepped benches, watering will be easier and you'll enjoy a nicer display area. Stepped benches also provide more room for plants than flat benches. However, they are somewhat more complicated to build.

In selecting the material from which to build your benches, you can choose from hardwood slat boards, which are strong and allow for good air circulation; cinderblocks with wooden boards set across them; or galvanized mesh on a wooden frame. Although hardwood slat benches are attractive, they do have a drawback that galvanized mesh does not. The orchids' roots attach themselves to the wood and can be damaged easily if they are removed from the slats; roots don't attach themselves to the galvanized mesh.

The strikingly beautiful Paphiopedilum phillipinense *'Red Corkscrew' is a must-have for all orchid lovers. It's a reliable, multiflowering bloomer when it reaches maturity.*

Watering

Determining the amount of water your orchids need is one of the most difficult aspects of orchid growing. You will have to pay close attention to your plants, whether you are growing them in a greenhouse, under lights or on a windowsill. When starting out, set aside a specific time each day to look at your plants. Feel the pots. Are they light and dry or heavy with water? Once in a while, tap the plants out of their pots and check the roots. Are they white and healthy looking or mushy and soft? Judge carefully the amount of water your orchids need. As a rule of thumb, water them more heavily in spring and summer and less often in fall and winter.

Misting your orchids during the hot days of summer generally is beneficial as it increases the humidity. However, there are certain orchids whose leaves become spotted and permanently marred when misted, so research your plants first before spritzing them.

Don't use a straight nozzle from a garden hose to water your orchids. The water stream is much too strong for your plants. It can knock them off their benches, throw them out of their pots and disturb their roots. Instead, use a spray or misting attachment. If you have selected your greenhouse flooring material wisely, you'll be able to water thoroughly and evenly, and any cleanup needed will be a simple matter. Concrete, brick, slate, gravel with stepping stones and

treated wood are all good flooring material. The advantages of gravel and brick are that they usually drain very easily.

Above all, keep your greenhouse growing area as clean as possible. Check your plants every day if possible and look for signs of pests and disease. Observe whether the plants are happy where they're placed. Your close attention to these details will ensure a glorious greenhouse filled with beautiful, blooming orchids throughout the year.

A profusion of orchids in the Cattleya alliance are growing beautifully at JEM nursery in Florida.

THE ORCHID GROWING GUIDE

Just a little information will help you immeasurably in expertly growing whatever variety of orchid you choose. All new orchid growers need to know how to get an orchid to grow well, put out healthy new roots, flower as often as possible, and ultimately reach specimen size. First, you must know your plant. When you add a new orchid to your collection, find out about the native habitat of the plant—at what temperatures it thrives and blooms, how humid the conditions are, and whether the plant grows in a sunny or shady location. The suggestions given here provide basic information, but remember that all rules have exceptions. The simple message is: Get to know your plants.

POTTING MEDIA

If you like to water your plants every day, make sure that the roots are in an airy mixture, such as bark with perlite, so they can dry somewhat between waterings. If you water less often, the potting medium you choose might include New Zealand sphagnum moss, which retains water longer. As most orchids in the wild do not grow in soil, you may wonder what types of potting mixtures are to be recommended. Many commercially prepared mixtures are available for orchids. Some orchid growers prefer to grow all of their plants in fir bark because it is inexpensive, easy to use and readily available, but there are numerous choices. What is most important is that the medium should have a loose composition and be able to retain water and nutrients. When choosing a potting medium for your orchid plants, remember that the thicker the orchid roots, the coarser the medium should be. You might like to try adding perlite or styrene chips to whatever potting medium you choose to assist in aeration. Here are the most commonly used orchid media, in addition to commercial orchid potting mixtures.

Fir Bark: You can buy fir bark in fine, medium and coarse grades. Fine-grade fir bark, consisting of ⅛- to ¼-inch pieces, is used primarily for seedlings or Miltonias and other orchids with very fine roots. Medium-grade fir bark, in ¼- to ½-inch pieces, is the fir bark most often used and is particularly good for epiphytic orchids. Coarse-grade fir bark, in ½- to 1-inch pieces, is best for Vandas and mature Phalaenopsis. It is not advisable to use ungraded fir bark when potting your plants. The finer pieces can block the spaces needed by the roots for aeration. You can use fir bark by itself, or add perlite to the mixture to increase water retention. Note: Prior to its use, fir bark should be thoroughly soaked.

Tree Fern: After fir bark, tree fern is the next most popular potting medium for orchids. This coarse material (it looks like little black sticks) is good for improving the aeration of pot-

At a Greater New York Orchid Show, a viewer stops to admire a spectacular display of Phalaenopses. Notice the traditional white and lavendar Phalaenopsis, as well as the yellow and art shade Phalaenopsis flowers that represent newer breeding trends.

A Phalaenopsis violacea *var. Borneo, beautifully grown, offers shiny green, slightly drooping leaves, successive blooming flowers and, adding to this orchid's incredible appeal, very fragrant flowers.*

Potting Tips

♦ *Try to stick with just one mix. It takes from approximately 9 months to a year to determine how the roots of a specific orchid react to a particular mix.*

♦ *It's best to repot between late winter and early spring.*

♦ *If your orchid has lost many of its roots, cut off the dead and rotted roots. Repot the orchid into a smaller pot. This makes watering easier and the media won't stay wet as long.*

♦ *Repot only a few orchids at a time, so you can give full attention to what you're doing.*

♦ *Repot only after flowering.*

♦ *Make sure your orchid is secure in its pot. If too loosely potted, it won't produce a good root system and will take a long time to establish itself.*

ting media. It is used extensively in the southern states, where it withstands the high humidity and high temperatures much better than fir bark. Tree fern provides excellent aeration for orchid roots and resists decay. It is more expensive than fir bark, but less expensive than osmunda fiber. If you don't water your plants very often, tree fern may not be the best potting medium for you, as you have to water tree fern about twice as often as you do fir bark. One orchidist suggests mixing tree fern with coarse or medium fir bark so it doesn't have to be watered quite as often.

Osmunda Fiber: The tried-and-true, longtime orchid medium is osmunda fiber, which consists of the roots of the royal fern (*Osmunda regalis*) and the spotted fern (*Polypodium*). However, osmunda fiber has become somewhat difficult to obtain nowadays and is extremely expensive when it is available. Orchid growers have found that fir bark is as good a medium, if not better; it is easier to handle and much less expensive.

New Zealand Sphagnum Moss: New Zealand sphagnum moss is a soft, spongy material

A close-up of a Vanda, showing the fan-shaped leaves. Note the growth habit of the roots, which are ambling out of the pot.

Although Vandas are typically warm-climate orchids, one of the best Vanda and Ascocenda growers in the country, Marilyn Mirro, does her growing in the Northeast, on Long Island.

that can hold up to 10 times its weight in water, a capacity that greatly exceeds that of any other potting medium for orchids. Another advantage of using sphagnum moss is that it naturally contains an antiseptic, which prevents damping off (rot) in orchid seedlings. Most orchid growers use only New Zealand sphagnum moss. Quite truthfully, I don't know any orchid growers—hobbyists or commercial growers—who use any other sphagnum moss. However, in my research I have seen descriptions of potting media that make reference to the generic term "sphagnum moss" as an important choice for orchid growers.

The intricate details of a Brassavola nodosa *flower show the barring on the orchid and the spiderlike appearance.*

Several types of New Zealand sphagnum moss are available: short- and long-fibered, as well as live and dried moss. The best moss for use with orchids is live sphagnum. When not overfertilized or too heavily watered, this moss will continue growing in the pot. It can be used alone, which many orchid growers do (particularly for Phalaenopsis and vandaceous orchids), or it can be used in combination with other media to provide added moisture retention. When working with sphagnum moss, it's suggested that rubber gloves be worn. Occasionally a fungus that exists in the moss is transmitted to a person.

Charcoal: Charcoal is not used alone as a potting medium, but as an additive to potting mixtures. It "sweetens" potting media by filtering out impurities. It lasts forever, as it does not break down.

Baskets: Many orchids are grown in baskets. Baskets made of redwood slats are particularly suitable for orchids with stems that are arching or pendulous. However, if an orchid has inflorescences that grow down through the medium, a basket made of chicken wire would be best. Orchids that need a thorough drying out between waterings do very well in baskets, which may be made of teak, cedar, redwood, plastic or wire mesh. Baskets come in many sizes and shapes; traditionally they are square, often octagonal, and range from about 4 inches to 18 inches across. Orchid supply companies, such as those listed at the back of this book, offer a good selection of baskets.

Shown here are the roots of a very healthy orchid. Notice the white velamen covering the roots and the green tips.

WATERING

Water is the main component of all plants. It dissolves and transports chemicals and is responsible for plant turgor and osmotic pressure. Nothing is more critical to a plant than water.

The watering of orchids is a very individual matter, but there are guidelines that can be followed. During the warmer months in spring, summer and early fall, water should be freely given. During the cooler, overcast days of winter, water less often. Always take care to ensure that your plants don't sit in water and that the roots have ample opportunity to dry out. If you're ever in doubt about watering, don't. Err on the side of dryness. More orchids die from overwatering than from any other cause.

Many orchids are epiphytes and can be found in rain forests growing on trees and not in soil. Rather than drawing moisture from soil, these orchids have adapted to their environment by developing roots that can absorb and retain whatever water falls on them. A spongy white material known as velamen envelops the roots and retains the water until it is used by the pseudobulbs and the leaves. (A pseudobulb is a thickened bulblike stem in some orchids where moisture is stored; unlike a true bulb, which is made up of layers, a pseudobulb is solid.)

Velamen is necessary for orchids in the wild. But in our homes, and with gardeners' tendencies to overwater their plants, the same velamen that conserves precious water in the wild can hold too much water for the orchids in our collections. Water prudently.

When should you water? The $64,000 Question. There is no one correct answer and there seem to be as many successful approaches to watering as there are orchid lovers. Some orchid varieties require more water than others. Some orchids require a rest period after blooming, during which water is withheld until new growth begins. Be sure to refer to the Orchid Portraits, where the watering requirements of individual plants are discussed.

Those orchids grown in clay pots tend to dry out more quickly than orchids grown in

A very easy-to-grow and easy-to-bloom orchid for the beginner is Blc. Toshi Aoki 'Pizazz' × Blc. Richard Mueller, shown growing and flowering in my yard during the summer. This little orchid also blooms in the fall.

Hints for Watering Orchids

♦ *If you've recently repotted your orchids, give them more water than you give to orchids that have been growing in the same pot for a while. Air spaces in the potting mix decrease and more water is retained as the potting medium ages and breaks down.*

♦ *To prevent disease, always aim to water your plants in the early part of the day so that water doesn't remain on the orchid after the sun goes down and the temperature drops. Watering in the morning will allow enough time for the moisture to evaporate.*

♦ *Water less often when the days are cool and cloudy, more often on hot and sunny days.*

♦ *Many experienced orchid growers can tell if their plants need watering by feeling the pot. If the pot feels relatively heavy, it's probably not in need of water. If the pot feels light, watering is probably needed.*

♦ *Orchids in clay pots dry out more quickly than those in plastic pots. Small pots need to be watered more frequently than larger pots.*

♦ *It's particularly important to water orchids in the Miltonia family on a steady basis. If watering is neglected, the orchid leaves assume an accordion-type pleating, demonstrating neglect.*

♦ *If the newest pseudobulb on your orchid has a shriveled rather than smooth, plump appearance, the plant is not getting enough water.*

Vanda Snow Angel depicts a variety of Vanda less often seen than the more traditional deep purple, blue or raspberry shades. This variety is white with just a mere shading of pale yellow.

When space is limited, mounting orchids as seen in this photo provides a great deal of space. This photograph was taken at Planting Fields Arboretum on Long Island, New York.

plastic pots. If your plants are receiving a great deal of light, obviously they will dry out faster than those in more shaded areas.

One simple way to see if watering is required is carefully to poke a pencil or your fingertip deep into the pot. If you detect water near the roots, although the top is bone dry, wait a few days and then test again. If your orchid is epiphytic with pseudobulbs and succulent leaves, don't water it until the medium is very dry right down to the bottom of the pot. Phalaenopsis, Paphiopedilums and Phragmipediums don't have pseudobulbs or very succulent leaves and should not be allowed to dry out between waterings. Vandas and other vandaceous orchids, such as Ascocendas and plants that are grown in baskets, need frequent watering. These orchids fare best when watered at least once a day, several times a day during the hot, dry days of summer.

Some very organized orchid growers group their orchids by size of pot, type of planting medium, whether the pots are clay or plastic or if the orchids are mounted. If you are similarly inclined, this may help you with your watering. Many epiphytic orchids do quite well by being mounted on a slab of tree fern or on a piece of cork bark, as their roots are then entirely free to dangle in the air as they would in nature. To mount an orchid, center the plant on the slab and place some New Zealand sphagnum moss around its roots. Attach the orchid to the mount with fine fishing line or, if this is not available, an old nylon stocking cut into strips can be used. It should be noted that orchids growing on mounts need to be watered more often than those in pots.

An absolutely wonderful orchid for beginners and advanced orchid growers alike, Brassavola nodosa has a very distinctive flower and can be grown either mounted or in a pot.

Here is an orchid that exemplifies a great beginner's orchid. Look at the size of the clay pot—it is only 4 inches. Look at the profusion of bright red, beautifully formed flowers it produces. The added benefit is that it blooms several times a year when given good light. This is my plant, and I anxiously await its bloom every few months.

AIR

Another vital factor for orchids is air, which must be available to the roots and surfaces of the plants. If the roots sit in water for too long without the opportunity to dry out, their inner portions rot because they are deprived of air. Air exchange is vital to orchids, epiphytic orchids in particular.

On a windowsill or under lights, you can very easily achieve good air circulation through the use of fans, positioned to blow gently on the orchids. Don't place the fans where they can damage the plants or blow too harshly; set them far enough from the orchids to provide a gentle breeze and good air movement. Your fans serve a dual purpose: not only do they promote good growth but they also prevent fungus and rot from destroying your plants. The temperature in your growing area will remain more stable because fans circulate the air, stirring up any humid air pockets that might promote fungal rot.

In my basement, I have two large light tables. I find that a four-foot oscillating fan placed about two feet away from the two tables provides the air circulation my orchids need. The many orchids that grow on my windowsill don't seem to require any fans at all, although I could use a small oscillating fan if it seemed necessary; the air in my basement seems considerably more stagnant and humid than the air in my livingroom.

One of my favorite orchids, it initially bloomed on my south-facing window. Now it has grown into a considerably larger plant in my greenhouse. In addition to the absolutely magnificent flowers, this Columbian Miltonia Hurricane Ridge 'Sylvia' is exceptionally fragrant as well. What more could one want in an orchid?

LIGHT

For most orchid genera, bright light is a requisite for healthy growth. Some plants, particularly those that are vandaceous (that is, members of the Vanda family), need very bright light to flourish and bloom. Others, such as Phalaenopsis and Paphiopedilums, can grow well in relatively low-light conditions. However, even those considered intermediate growers need bright, diffuse light to produce flowers. Unless you plan to grow orchids under lights, look for the brightest spot you can find because, although there are exceptions, this is the best situation for most of the orchids you will probably want to grow.

The ideal location is a south-facing window. Here, you must be careful your orchids don't burn during the heat of the day and in the hot summer months. When in bloom, your orchids should be moved away or shielded from the light; if their exposure isn't moderated, the flowers will not be as long-lived and will fade quickly. Sheer curtains, blinds or whitewash paint on the panes will prevent this problem. Many orchids will do well in an east- or west-facing window. If in doubt about the quantity of light in a particular growing area, consult a light meter (see page 13).

Your plants will let you know if they are getting enough light. If the leaves are dark

Light for Your Orchids

♦ *The correct amount of light is vital to successful orchid growing.*

♦ *If orchid leaves are very yellow, they are probably getting too much sun. If dark green, they are probably not getting enough.*

♦ *To keep your orchids from producing lopsided growth, rotate their pots every other time you water. However, don't turn your orchids when they're in bud. The flowers will turn to face the sun, resulting in a skewed display on the stem.*

♦ *Observe a newly acquired orchid plant carefully to see that it isn't getting too much light. When a plant is moved from one location to another, it needs time to adjust to the new surroundings. Gradually increase the amount of light you are giving your new orchid so that the leaves don't burn.*

♦ *It's a good idea to wipe off the leaves of your orchids so they get the maximum benefits from sunlight. If dust and dirt accumulate, the amount of light they receive is diminished.*

♦ *If you suspect your plants are getting too much sun, touch the leaves. If they feel hot, move the plants to an area where there's less light.*

♦ *When growing orchids on a windowsill, place those that need the most sun closest to the window. Those needing less can be placed farther away from the window.*

♦ *When the buds of your orchid are opening, move the orchid away from the strongest area of light. Too much sunlight will make the flowers wilt faster and lose some of their color.*

Ascocenda John De Biase can be found in several shades. This particular cultivar is very dark in color. I found it relatively easy to get this orchid to bloom in my basement, at the center of my light table. To ensure this plant would get maximum light, I placed it on top of an inverted pot to raise it up even closer to the light.

Fertilizing Techniques

♦ *Always make sure that the potting medium has been thoroughly watered before applying fertilizer. Otherwise, the roots of the orchid will burn. The water in the medium helps dilute the fertilizer.*

♦ *As with watering, use less fertilizer rather than more. Too much is not a good thing.*

♦ *When applying fertilizer, always decrease the concentration amount recommended in the directions.*

♦ *Never fertilizer an orchid that has damaged roots, or one that isn't entirely healthy. Fertilizer should be used only in diluted form on strong, growing plants.*

♦ *If the leaf tips of your orchids are black and look dry, stop your fertilizer program. Cut off the damaged portion of the leaves, making sure to sterilize the scissors between cuts. It's recommended that you leach the potting medium by a thorough watering so that no extra fertilizer remains. If you notice the plant doesn't appear to improve and that dry and blackened leaf tips remain after leaching, you may want to remove the entire plant and repot it (see page 45).*

The leaves of Phalaenopsis schilleriana *are thought by many to be the most attractive part of this orchid. This orchid, easy to grow for most beginners, has a very floriferous nature as well.*

green, there isn't enough light; if they are yellowish green, there is too much light. Medium green, firm leaves are ideal. Consistent blooming is another indication the plants are getting ample light. Here are a few important "dos and dont's": Don't expose seedlings or newly planted orchids to the direct sun of a southern exposure. Do turn your orchids at least once a week so they grow evenly. Don't, however, change the direction the plant is facing when it is in bud; the flowers and spike will grow twisted.

FERTILIZER

Because most orchid potting media have no nutrients, your orchids need fertilizer. In nature, epiphytes garner nutrients from organic matter decaying near their roots. Terrestrial orchids get nutrients from organic matter in the soil. Whether you grow your orchids on a windowsill, under lights or in a greenhouse, you should follow nature's example as closely as possible in providing nutrients for your plants.

Orchids in the wild are not inundated with a massive dose

of fertilizer one week and then deprived of fertilizer for the next three weeks; they make use of dilute amounts of nutrients every day. You can help your orchids do the same thing by giving them a very weak solution of fertilizer regularly. Many professional orchid growers recommend applying liquid fertilizer in a very weak solution each time you water for three weeks, and during the fourth week use no fertilizer (but water thoroughly to leach out high concentrations of minerals and salts remaining in the pot).

It's a good idea to water your plants very thoroughly the day before you fertilize them so the roots are not damaged. This can happen if fertilizer is applied to a dry plant. Watering first also allows an even distri-bution of the fertilizer throughout the pot.

There are many fertilizers on the market today. The components of a commercial fertilizer are described by three numbers in a sort of shorthand, always representing the relative percentages of nitrogen (N), phosphorus (P) and potassium (K). For example, a fertilizer formula of 20-20-20 contains 20 percent nitrogen, 20 percent phosphorus and 20 percent potassium, plus such trace minerals as zinc and iron that are needed by plants, but in smaller amounts.

Your choice of fertilizer depends upon the medium in which you are growing your orchids. If you are using fir bark, apply the fertilizer formula 30-10-10 because fir bark decomposes very rapidly, and this leaves the growing medium nitrogen poor; 30-10-10 fertilizer will compensate for this deficiency. Orchids potted in other media are well served by such fertilizer formulas as 20-20-20 and 18-18-18, containing equal amounts of nitrogen, phosphorus and potassium. After new growth is complete, many experienced orchid growers change their formula to 10-30-20, which acts as a blossom booster. When it comes to fertilizers, remember to use only a dilute fertilizer on a regular basis. If the tips of the leaves turn black, you are overfertilizing. Giving extra fertilizer won't produce larger, more spectacular flowers; instead, it will burn the leaves and set the plant back. Here, too much of a good thing is really detrimental.

POTS

The choice of container in which to grow your orchid is a personal one. However, it is practical for the beginning orchid grower, unsure about how often to water or what type of container or growing medium is best, to keep a new plant in the container it was grown in for some time before changing to a new container. (Most orchids today are sold in plastic pots.)

If you water your plants very often or very heavily, consider clay pots, as they tend to dry out more quickly than others. Plastic pots are lighter, retain water more easily, and are less expensive. Plastic pots have the added advantage of not retaining salts, and if the water is hard where you live, you should certainly use plastic pots. Salt residues from hard water linger in clay pots and can burn the roots of your orchid.

Some orchids don't like to be potted at all, preferring to grow epiphytically as they do in nature, mounted on a slab or hanging in a slatted basket. Generally, these orchids won't survive the moisture that accu-mulates in a pot. If your orchid is one that should be mounted, there are various materials to choose among for the "slab," including cork, tree fern and wood. (You can even mount the orchid on branches to imitate its growth in nature.) To mount an orchid, center the plant on the slab, place some New Zealand sphagnum moss around the roots, and attach it to the mount by using strips of soft cloth or old stockings, or very fine gauge fishing wire.

A close-up of one of the most attractive orchids—Brassavola nodosa. *This is my plant, and I prefer to grow it mounted, although many growers prefer growing it in a pot.*

A wonderful specimen of a Brazilian Miltonia is shown here. Notice the many large flowers, deep purple in the dorsal, sepals and petals, and the contrasting, lightly veined lip of Miltonia spectabilis *var.* moreliana.

HOW TO REPOT YOUR ORCHID

One of the first things a new orchid grower should realize is that when an orchid is to be repotted, all of the "old" potting medium around the roots and in the pot should be removed. When you have finished freeing the roots, they should be bare. This is done so that no remaining potting mixture, which has decomposed, will promote rot and injure the roots.

Before you repot, water the plant thoroughly to make the roots wet and more pliable. Also make sure that the fresh potting mix has been thoroughly soaked, preferably overnight. If you are using a tree fern or bark mix, any tiny particles that could clog the air spaces in the mix will sink in the soaking water, and the larger pieces—which you'll use to pot your orchid—will float to the top.

Remove the plant from the old pot: Place the pot on its side and pull the orchid out by grabbing the base of the plant. If the plant doesn't come out of the pot easily, set it upright again and gently run a sharp knife with a long blade around the inside edge of the pot. Then, try removing the plant again by turning the pot on its side and tugging. If all else fails, break the pot and remove the plant. Remove all of the old medium carefully with your fingers and by gently shaking the plant. Whatever potting mixture remains at this point can be removed by running it under water.

Don't divide your plant unless it is growing in an asymetrical fashion. To pot a monopodial orchid, such as an Ascocenda, hold it in one hand and place it in the center of the pot; fill in with potting medium around the base of the plant and the roots, tamping it down with your fingers as you work. Add your mix until it reaches the bottom of the lowest leaf. Tamp the mixture down again by banging the entire pot down on a table. With sympodial orchids, the method differs. You're not going to center your plant, but rather position the old pseudobulbs against one side of the pot, leaving enough room in the pot for new pseudobulbs to form and grow. As you fill the pot with the potting mixture, continue tamping it down. When the pot is full, bang the pot on a sturdy surface so that it settles.

Repotting an orchid is relatively easy. Once you learn that you don't have to wear kid gloves to handle an orchid, you'll become adept at repotting. One cautionary note: Make sure that the plant is secure in the pot. If the plant is wobbly, the roots will be damaged and the health of the plant jeopardized.

ORCHID GROWING FOR PRESENTATION AND JUDGING

There are many opportunities for you to show off your beautifully grown orchids. Each month your local orchid society probably has a meeting. Some areas have several local orchid societies, so you could attend three or four meetings every month, if you were so inclined. At most of these meetings there is a sales table where vendors bring wonderful orchids for you to buy. There's a show table set up, too, where you can exhibit your plants for others to see and for judges within the club to assess.

In front of each exhibitor's area will be a card. On the lower part of the card (turned under, so the judges are not prejudiced), you write your name, the class in which your plant is eligible (see below) and the date. On the upper part of the card you list every plant that you've brought to the meeting to be judged. When the judges (generally two or three) assess a plant, they give

it a rating from 1 to 10. Orchids are judged on flower quality, flower color, good culture, whether a good grouping of similar plants is provided, and on the rarity of the orchid. Points are awarded, taking all of these factors into account. Whenever you bring plants to the show table, you receive points.

If your orchid entry was grown on a windowsill or under lights, it is in Class A; in a small greenhouse, Class B; in a larger greenhouse, Class C. Professional growers compete in Class D. Whenever you win first place in your class you automatically are moved into the next class, for example, from A into B, B into C, and so on. Then, at the end of the year, the points are counted and the results compared. The individual in your club (or clubs) who has the most points gets first place in his or her class; the individual with the second most points is awarded second place, and third place goes to the third highest number of points. As there are often several hundred members in each club, winning one of the top three awards is quite an accomplishment.

This is local club judging.

To go one step farther, there is official American Orchid Society judging on a regular basis. Here your plants are judged by AOS-certified judges. It should be noted that the purpose of judging orchids is to promote and recognize new and superior forms of orchids through orchid breeding. AOS judges are expected to be aware of breeding trends.

In judging, the AOS allocates 30 percent of the total score for flower form, ideally full, round and symmetrical, with each of the segments equal. Another 30 percent is allotted to flower color, which should be clear, bright and even throughout the flower. The remaining points are given for flower size (which should be at least equal to the average of both of the parent orchids), gloss, firm texture and good substance.

The spike and appearance of the flowers on the stem are important, too. If the spike is twisted, or the flowers unevenly arranged or turning in different directions, points will be deducted. Another consideration is the number of flowers on the plant. A multiflowering orchid such as an *Odontoglossum* would need many flowers to

gain an award. However, a *Paphiopedilum* with only one flower could easily garner one. Finally, the stem's length in portion to the plant size is judged. When a plant is awarded, a photograph is taken of the plant so that it's permanently recorded. Most judging societies produce a book, whether on a quarterly, monthly or annual basis, listing all the orchids that were awarded for that period.

American Orchid Society Awards

FIRST CLASS CERTIFICATE—FCC/AOS: an orchid receiving between 90 and 100 points in judging.

AWARD OF MERIT—AM/AOS: an orchid receiving between 80 and 89 points in judging.

HIGH CLASS CERTIFICATE—HCC/AOS: an orchid receiving between 75 and 79 points.

Other American Orchid Society Awards:
  AWARD OF QUALITY—AQ/AOS
  JUDGES' COMMENDATION—JC/AOS
  CERTIFICATE OF BOTANICAL RARITY—CBR/AOS
  CERTIFICATE OF CULTURAL MERIT—CCM/AOS
  CERTIFICATE OF HORTICULTURAL MERIT—CHM/AOS

Another strikingly beautiful Miltonia, this one is the cooler growing Columbian type, commonly referred to as the pansy orchid. Looking at this photograph, one can readily see that Miltonia 'Paradise Park Mighty Waters' resembles a pansy.

Here's one of the most beautiful orchids. The clear reddish orange petals and sepals contrast magnificently with the golden yellow lip. Wilsonara Harlequin 'Redrock' will bloom on a windowsill or under lights. However, after the spike begins growing, your Wilsonaras should be moved to an area where there's room for inflorescence to grow.

Opposite: Doritis pulcherrima 'Frank' is a beautiful orchid for the beginner, with richly colored flowers, attractively presented on long inflorescences.

Right: Oncidiums are a delightful group of orchids for beginners to grow. Although the flowers are generally small, the plants are very floriferous and easily grown into specimen size.

ORCHID PORTRAITS

These portraits will introduce you to the easiest of orchids to grow. They are identified either as Easy or Slightly Difficult. To provide you with information about the cultural requirements to succeed with your orchid, I have outlined the light, temperature and color for each of the 40 orchids. If there is something additional that will help you succeed with growing and blooming your orchids, I've included this fact in the plant portraits as well. For instance, certain orchids grow better in baskets than in pots, some need a very coarse potting mixture, and others require a rest period after blooming.

PLANT PORTRAIT KEY

Here is a guide to the symbols and terms used throughout this section.

Light Requirements:

○ indicates the orchid requires high light, equivalent to full sun
◑ indicates the orchid will bloom in intermediate light, which may be bright, diffuse light or half shade
● indicates the orchid requires low or indirect light

Although some orchid cultural guides describe the amount of light an orchid genus needs in terms of footcandles, in my opinion (and that of many other orchid growers) it is much more important to observe how your plants fare in different light situations. Look at the leaves, for instance. If they are very yellow, they are getting too much light; if they are dark green, they aren't getting enough.

Temperature Requirements: Temperature ranges listed refer to evening temperatures.

W indicates a preference for warm growing conditions, 65° to 70° F.
I indicates a preference for intermediate growing conditions, 55° to 65° F.
C indicates a preference for cool to cold growing conditions, 45° to 55° F.

Angraceum sesquipedale (an-GRAY-kom), Easy. ◑
Temperature: I
Colors: White, white with green
Characteristics: Within this species of orchid are more than 200 varieties. Angraceums are epiphytic plants native to Africa and the island of Madagascar. The flowers are always either creamy white or white with green. Nearly all varieties produce flowers with a long spur, or nectary, from the back of the lip.

Angraceums can be grown on windowsills (particularly the smaller varieties, such as *Angraceum leonis* and *Angraceum phillipinense*). If you have adequate room you can successfully grow an *Angraceum sesquipedale* as pictured here or a beautiful hybrid, *Angraceum eburneum.*
Cultural Information: Angraceums grow best in indirect sunlight. They bloom best when given night temperatures of 55° to 60° F. and daytime temperatures of 65° to 75° F. Angraceums can be grown in pots, in baskets with osmunda or tree fern chunks, and on cork slabs. They should be kept moist at all times. Good drainage is very important, and a humidity level of 60 percent is preferable. When growing An-

Oncidium Sharri Baby is another wonderful beginner's orchid. Not only are the soft, muted colors beautiful, but the many flowers produced are very fragrant.

The large, waxy, greenish white flowers of Angraceum sesquipedale *stand out beautifully against the dark green, fan-shaped leaves.*

For those who love the look of a Vanda, and the large Vandaceous-type flowers, but who cannot accommodate these very large plants, Ascocenda Butterfly is a wonderful alternative with large, clear red flowers.

graceums in fir bark or in pots, use a 30-10-10 fertilizer; when growing them on a mount, use an 18-18-18 formula. As with other orchids, always dilute your fertilizer to half strength.

Ascocenda (as-co-SEN-da) 'Butterfly', Easy. ○
Temperature: W
Color: Red
Characteristics: Ascocenda 'Butterfly', an incredibly beautiful hybrid, will bloom for you if given a sunny location in a south-facing window or a place near and toward the middle of your fluorescent lights. Not only are the flowers a beautifully bright, true red color, but they are also quite large—3 to 5 inches—and flat, a delight to behold. When mature, Ascocenda 'Butterfly' rewards you with six to ten flowers on each spike.
Cultural Information: Grow your Ascocendas in a basket. Give them lots of dilute fertil-

izer on a rectangular basis and provide them with as much humidity as you can. Use a humidifier, place your Ascocendas among other plants, and mist them. Under conditions such as these, you will have an incredibly beautiful basketful of vibrant red flowers.

Ascocenda miniatum, Easy. ○
Temperature: W
Color: Orange
Characteristics: Ascocenda miniatum is a wonderful plant for the beginning orchid grower. If you can provide good light, preferably near a south- or east-facing window, or a good position under lights or in a greenhouse, this small plant will reward you by covering itself with diminutive, vibrant orange flowers. Ascocenda miniatum is a monopodial plant with flowers that open in succession. They are usually flat and each has a spur. Given good cul-

Here's a collection of Ascocenda miniatums, very short growing orchids. They are best grown in baskets and are easy to bloom on a windowsill, under lights and in a greenhouse. The vivid orange color and cluster of tiny flowers will provide you with a plant that remains in bloom for months.

ture, it will become a specimen plant in no time.

Cultural Information: Best planted in baskets in a loose potting mix made up of fir bark, charcoal and pieces of crockery, or in New Zealand sphagnum moss, *A. miniatum* needs a very thorough drenching so that the velamen covering the roots becomes green; then, it requires exposure to the air so they dry out. For this reason, baskets are preferred to pots for this orchid. *A. miniatum* can also be grown quite well mounted. As with other vandaceous types, don't repot this orchid; once the roots have filled the basket, merely place it, basket and all, into a larger basket.

Blc. Richard Mueller × self, Easy. ◑ ○

Temperature: I
Color: Yellowish orange with red
Characteristics: This is a good example of a Cattleya-type orchid. It is a small plant that

will provide you with six or seven delicate, yellowish orange flowers with fine red spotting on the lips. The flowers are relatively small, but this compact plant blooms so often—sometimes three or four times a year—that it epitomizes the saying "good things come in small packages." Several well-known nurseries offer this plant in their catalogues. It is inexpensive and offers instant gratification. "Blc." refers to the fact that this genus is a combination of *Brassia, Laelia* and *Cattleya.*

Cultural Information: Grow in an epiphytic potting mix. Give good light and moderate humidity. Will flower best when somewhat potbound. Fertilize every week (use a weak solution of 20-20-20, or 30-10-10 if you're growing this orchid in fir bark) for three weeks; then, for the fourth week, don't fertilize—just water thoroughly so that any remaining fertilizer and mineral salts will be leached out.

Blc. Toshi Aoki 'Pizazz' × *Blc.* Richard Mueller, Easy. ◑ ○

Temperature: I
Colors: Cream shades to yellow with red splashes and tips.
Characteristics: Here is another Cattleya-type orchid that is exceptionally easy for the new orchidist to grow and bloom. Unlike the larger Cattleyas you will find in this chapter, *Blc. Toshi Aoki* 'Pizazz' × *Blc.* Richard Mueller is a miniature Cattleya that will bloom for you several times a year. Like *Slc. Regal Gold* 'Laina' (page 70), this little plant never grows to more than 8 to 10 inches high. Yet it will reward you with an abundance of flowers that range from light cream to yellow to yellow with red tips and striping, and many are spotted in the lip.
Cultural Information: Blc. Toshi Aoki 'Pizazz' × *Blc.* Richard Mueller came to me in a two-inch pot, and it bloomed in this tiny pot with three perfect flowers. As the plant grew and was repotted, flower number and size increased. This plant does well in a plastic or clay pot with fine fir bark, charcoal and perlite mix.

Here's a close-up of Blc. Toshi Aoki 'Pizazz' × Blc. Richard Mueller mentioned previously. Notice the number of beautiful flowers on this miniature Cattleya growing in a 3-inch clay pot.

Blc. Richard Mueller × self will delight every beginning orchid grower. It is exceptionally easy to bring into bloom and produces many flowers, even on a young plant.

Brassavola digbyana *when in bloom just cannot be ignored by anyone who sees it. The magnificent lip, which is markedly fimbriated, is the most outstanding feature of this large-flowered orchid.*

Brassavola digbyana

(brah-sa-VOL-a), Easy. ◐ ○
Temperature: I to W
Color: Greenish yellow
Characteristics: Brassavolas are easy plants for the novice orchid grower. *Brassavola digbyana* grows naturally in Mexico and Central America where conditions are warm and somewhat dry. It is one of the most strikingly beautiful of all the Brassavolas. Its most outstanding feature, a very large, fimbriated (frilly) lip, gives an extremely distinctive appearance to the flower. The petals are a greenish yellow (some say chartreuse), and the flower is exceptionally large given the

Here's a closeup of the heart-shaped Brassavola nodosa *mentioned previously.*

size of the plant. *B. digbyana*, like *Cattleya walkeriana alba* 'Pendentive', is often used in hybridization for its large flower size, fimbriated lip and good vigor. It should be grown by everyone who can get one. These plants will bloom in a south-facing window or under lights, and they impart a wonderful fragrance. They also have the advantage of needing less humidity than many other orchids.
Cultural Information: Requiring basically the same growing conditions as Cattleyas, *Brassavola digbyana* doesn't need as much water, so don't keep it overly moist. It appreciates being placed in a bright area. Grow in plastic pots in an epiphytic mix, or mounted. After flowering, give this plant a rest: no fertilizer, less water. When actively growing, *B. digbyana* needs less water than *B. Nodosa*.

Brassavola nodosa,

Easy. ◐
Temperature: I
Colors: White, pale green
Characteristics: Originating from Panama, Venezuela and Mexico, *Brassavola nodosa* is one of the most fragrant of orchids. However, the scent is perceptible only in the evening, hence the nickname, "lady of the night." *B. nodosa* has medium-size pseudobulbs that produce inflorescences that hang down. For this reason, it is best grown either mounted or in a basket. The long-lasting flowers are white or a very pale green. The lip is white with a purple spot in the center. *B. nodosa* generally flowers more than once a

year, usually in spring and winter.
Cultural Information: When this plant is growing, make sure that it receives plenty of water. After flowering, don't stop watering entirely, but give just enough so the plant doesn't dry out.

Catasetum (cat-a-SEE-tum), 'White Knight', Easy. ◐ ○
Temperature: I to W
Color: White
Characteristics: Catasetums are wonderful and unusual orchids seen less frequently in orchid collections than some other genuses. They are quite varied in color. They are intriguing and quite easy for the beginning orchid grower. A unique feature of Catasetums is that when an insect steps on a triggering device in the Catasetum, the plant shoots pollen at the insect, which then carries it to another plant. These orchids

An example of a Catasetum *in bloom, this one at JEM nursery in Florida. Notice the pendulous spikes, which indicate that this plant often does best when in a basket.*

have large pseudobulbs and deciduous leaves. *Catasetum* 'White Knight' is a prolific hybrid that is relatively easy to bloom.

Cultural Information: Catasetums need bright light, good ventilation and intermediate to warm temperatures to bloom. They are wonderful for growing under lights if provided with good air circulation from fans. Catasetums need plenty of water when they are growing. However, when the leaves fall, stop watering almost entirely; provide only enough water so that the pseudobulbs don't shrivel up. In spring when growth begins anew, start watering on a regular basis again. Catasetums can be grown in pots or baskets as the flowers appear on pendulous inflorescences. Pot Catasetums either in tree fern fiber or osmunda.

Cattleya maxima (CAT-lee-ya), Easy. ○ ◑

Temperature: I
Color: Deep pink
Characteristics: There are about 50 species and thousands of hybrid Cattleyas. *C. maxima,* one of the most beautiful species, requires good light as all Cattleyas do. A southern or eastern exposure is preferred for windowsill culture. Cattleyas do exceptionally well under lights, too. As the plants mature, they will reward you with many beautiful flowers. Cattleyas have firm pseudobulbs. Depending on the number of leaves atop the pseudobulbs, Cattleyas are described as unifoliate (one leaf) or bifoliate (two leaves). Unifoliate Cattleyas have two to six

Cattleya maxima is a long-time favorite of orchid growers. Here is a wonderful specimen showing the beautiful pink color and heavily veined lip.

large, showy flowers. Bifoliate Cattleyas generally have more flowers, but they are usually smaller in size. Try *C. Maxima* if you are a beginner. It differs from the other Cattleya and Cattleya-type orchids I have discussed so far, in that it is a species Cattleya with a very large flower and makes a wonderful specimen plant.

Cultural Information: When potting Cattleyas you may use osmunda or fir bark. Some species can be grown mounted on tree fern or cork. Like several other orchid genuses, Cattleyas will bloom best when they are somewhat potbound. Cattleyas don't have soft leaves, so when the ambient temperature is high, misting benefits these orchids and doesn't adversely affect the leaves.

Cattleya maxima, like others in its genus, likes to be watered abundantly and then allowed to dry out. In cooler weather, water less and don't allow the

leaves to remain wet. (This is good advice for all orchids.) Water more heavily in sunny, warm weather and less on cool, gray or rainy days. Cattleyas need fertilization on a regular basis. Those grown in fir bark should be fertilized using a 30-10-10 formula. Those in tree fern or osmunda will benefit from a regular application of 20-20-20.

Cattleya walkeriana alba 'Pendentive', Easy. ○ ◑

Temperature: I
Color: White
Characteristics: Cattleyas and cattleya-type orchids are among the most beautiful of all orchids. They come in every conceivable color, and many are fragrant. They bloom reliably, and the miniature Cattleyas provide you with flowers two or even three times a year.

Cattleyas are exceptionally rewarding and can tolerate a

If you love pure white flowers, then this orchid is perfect for you. It's easy to grow and bloom, and the flowers are perfectly shaped.

great variety of growing conditions. By choosing a Cattleya, such as *C. walkeriana alba* 'Pendentive', you, the beginner, won't be frustrated by owning a plant that is in bloom when you purchase it, but never blooms again. This beautiful, large-flowered white orchid will grow and bloom easily for you, whether on a windowsill, under lights or in a greenhouse. Many outstanding Cattleya hybrids have been created using this orchid as one of the parents.

Cultural Information: Grow *Cattleya walkeriana alba* 'Pendentive' in good light. Keep it in small pots, as it produces flowers best when rootbound.

Cirrhopetalum (see-row-PET-a-lum), 'Elizabeth Anne Buckleberry', Easy to Slightly Difficult. ◐ ○

Temperature: I to W
Colors: White, tan, pale yellow
Characteristics: Cirrhopetalums are wonderful orchids for the beginner to try. As most species are small, they are ideal subjects for growing indoors, particularly under lights. Originally an Indian species, Cirrhopetalums have creeping rhizomes, very short stems and intricately patterned flowers in colors of white, tan or pale yellow, oftentimes marked with brown or red. *C.* 'Elizabeth Anne Buckleberry' has extremely beautiful flowers that are umbellate when mature, bearing a strong resemblance to umbrellas, as the adjective implies.

Cultural Information: Because the flowers are pendulous, I recommend that Cirrhopetalums be grown mounted on a tree fern slab or in a basket with New Zealand sphagnum moss. You might try growing *C.* 'Elizabeth Anne Buckleberry' in a small osmunda fiber basket.

Comparettia speciosa

(com-pah-RET-ee-a), Easy. ◐ ○
Temperature: I
Colors: Orange to yellow-orange
Characteristics: Here's a delightful, small orchid very easy to grow and bloom. *Comparettia speciosa* is one of about ten epiphytic species found in South America, near the Andes mountain range. Visitors to Ecuador and Peru have reported seeing these plants growing high in guava trees. The flowers are plentiful, borne on arching spikes. The leaves are large and leathery. In contrast, the

Cirrhopetalums—umbellate in appearance and pendulous— are exceptional orchids. Here's a close-up of Cirrhopetalum Elizabeth Ann Buckleberry. However, when the total plant is seen, a complete circle of flowers hangs down gracefully from the plant.

Comparettia speciosa *is a magnificent species with loads of beautiful orangish yellow flowers. Notice the very large lip on this plant.*

pseudobulbs are small and almost totally hidden by the foliage. The three best-known *Comparettia* species are *C. falcata*, *C. coccinea* and the one pictured here, *C. speciosa*. *C. coccinea* is red, *C. falcata* is dark rose and *C. speciosa* is orange to yellow-orange. All of these species are well worth acquiring.

Cultural Information: It is important to note, in growing Comparettias, that they need good air circulation and good light to thrive and bloom. Try positioning them in the path of an oscillating fan, in high light or in a central spot on your fluorescent light table. Comparettias can be grown in small pots of tree fern with New Zealand sphagnum moss added and on slabs.

This is a beautiful standard Cymbidium flower. If you're able to provide room for the tall spikes and oversize plant that a standard Cymbidium ultimately becomes, you should try Cymbidium Arroyo Seco 'Red Ruffle' with its deep red flowers edged in white.

Cymbidium (sim-BID-ee-um), Arroyo Seco 'Red Ruffle', Easy. ◑ ○

Temperature: C to I

Colors: Dark red with white

Characteristics: Most novice orchid growers are familiar with Cymbidiums because they are frequently used in orchid corsages. They are mass-produced by many commercial growers not only for corsages but also floral sprays; the plants provide a profusion of very showy, exceptionally long-lasting flowers. There may be as many as 30 to 35 flowers on one spike alone. The flowers can be found in every conceivable color, and they often have a lip of a contrasting color. To complete the picture, many Cymbidiums are fragrant.

At one time, Cymbidiums were not considered good plants for the beginning orchid grower because the standard type takes up a tremendous amount of room, more than can be accommodated under lights or on a windowsill. Cymbidiums used to be grown primarily by those with greenhouses. However, times have changed, and thanks to hybridization, miniature Cymbidiums such as *C. Arroyo Seco* 'Red Ruffle' are a wonderful addition to the collection of home orchid growers.

Cultural Information: Miniature Cymbidiums should be grown in pots, preferably in fir bark; use large chunks for large plants, finer bark for smaller plants putting out new growth. Don't repot them unless absolutely necessary. They bloom much better when they are pot-bound. Unlike standard Cymbidiums, miniature Cymbidiums should be watered continually with no rest period. Make sure that your Cymbidiums have enough light during the summer and into early fall so that the leaves actually turn yellow. Ensure that the plants receive adequate air circulation. Once you see buds forming on the plant, take it out of the bright sunlight and give it more shade. Once the flowers have finished blooming, put the plant back into full sunlight again.

Cymbidiums require a lot of fertilizer, particularly from January through July, when they should be given a liquid fertilizer every two weeks. From August through December, fertilize them about once a month. You may want to use a fertilizer formulated specifically for Cymbidiums.

Dendrobium Golden Sun is a short growing orchid that produces many small flowers, generally two times per year.

Dendrobium (den-DRO-bee-um), 'Golden Sun', Slightly Difficult. ◐ ○

Temperature: I
Color: Golden yellow
Characteristics: Dendrobiums are one of the most diverse orchid genuses. There are more than 1,500 species, and the many different types of Dendrobiums require different culture, originating as they do from around the world—Japan and Korea, India and Burma, Australia and New Zealand; New Guinea is especially rich in Dendrobium species. *D.* 'Golden Sun' is an evergreen variety that has pseudobulbs. Not all Dendrobiums have compact habits; some are several feet tall and therefore not suitable for growing under lights or on windowsills. This Dendrobium is compact enough to do well on a windowsill and particularly good for growing under lights. Grow Dendrobiums for their variety of colors, abundance of flowers and fragrance. However, some are more difficult to grow and flower than others, so choose carefully.

Cultural Information: Dendrobium 'Golden Sun' sheds some of its leaves in fall, when it needs a rest period. When new growth begins, resume watering. It can be grown in a pot with an epiphytic mixture with some New Zealand sphagnum moss added to improve moisture retention, or it can be grown mounted. Give this orchid good light.

Encyclia mariae (en-SIK-lee-a), Easy. ◐

Temperature: I to C
Colors: Lime green and white
Characteristics: As is the case with other orchids in my collection, *Encyclia mariae* never fails to astound me, my family and visitors with its beauty. *E. mariae* is a small, epiphytic plant with rather large pseudobulbs and bifoliate leaves. Peeking from among the leaves are several large, beautiful, lime green flowers, each with a huge white lip. *E. mariae* blooms during the summer, and the flowers last for a week or two. On a first-bloom seedling you will probably find only one flower, but as the plant matures it will produce three or four flowers at a time, making a lovely display. This fragrant orchid is native to Mexico, and like other Encyclias it is easy to grow and flower. Purchase

This is Encyclia mariae, *one of my personal favorites. Here is a close-up of the magnificent flower that has an amazing contrast of dark green sepals and petals and the white lip. I grow this plant mounted.*

Encyclias whenever you have the opportunity and the price is right. They are easy plants for beginners to grow and offer instant gratification.

Cultural Information: Although many people grow *Encyclia mariae* potted, mine is mounted on a piece of fir bark and hung on a shelf on my windowsill until I take all of my plants outdoors for the summer. After flowering, decrease the amount of water the plant receives. During winter, let it go rather dry.

Encyclia vitellina,
Easy. ○ ◑

Temperature: C to I
Color: Orange-red with yellow
Characteristics: Encyclia species number more than 240, and *E. vitellina* is one of the most colorful. Encyclias, which are epiphytic orchids, can be found throughout South and Central America; this species grows high in the mountains of Mexico and Guatemala. All members of the genus have pseudobulbs. They are wonderful plants for the novice orchid grower, although it should be noted that *Encyclia vitellina* requires cooler temperatures than some other species. When this plant is in bloom, it's a sight to behold with the brightest orange-red flowers imaginable, each flower made even more strikingly beautiful because of its vibrant yellow lip. Unlike some other Encyclias (see *E. mariae*, page 58), *E. vitellina* produces its flowers on an upright spike. The flowers generally number twenty or more to a spike when the plant is mature. Note that spikes may require staking.

Cultural Information: Like Cattleyas, Encyclias require good light and will do well either mounted or in a pot. Fertilize them every two to three weeks when they are growing. Give them less water and no fertilizer when they're at rest.

Lycaste (lie-KASS-tee) 'Peach Glow', Easy. ◑

Temperature: I
Color: Peach
Characteristics: There are approximately 45 varieties of Lycastes. *Lycaste* 'Peach Glow' is seen less frequently in collections than it should be, given the lush foliage and absolutely beautiful flowers it produces. Most Lycastes are epiphytic and are native to Latin and Central America, from Peru to Guatemala to Mexico. Lycastes have unique flowers, substantial, long lasting and triangular. 'Peach Glow' is a reliable bloomer and the soft color of the flowers is enchanting. These medium-size plants can be grown successfully without a greenhouse and can provide a great deal of satisfaction for the beginning orchidist. They should be grown in pots and should not be repotted too often; it's preferable to wait until the plant needs to be divided before repotting it. Lycastes generally flower in spring.

Cultural Information: Lycastes require abundant watering when they are actively growing. After flowering, let them rest and until new growth begins, without water almost to the point of dryness and at a lower temperature.

This Encyclia looks entirely different from Encyclia mariae. Encyclia vitelliana *produces smaller, more star-shaped, bright orange flowers with a narrow yellow lip. Again, this orchid is easy for the beginner to grow.*

Lycaste Peach Glow offers another very different type of orchid flower. At first glance, Lycaste flowers appear similiar in shape to tulips.

Admittedly one of the most striking of the Masdevallias, Copperwing almost seems to glow from within. It's an intermediate growing plant and should provide the beginner with a small plant covered with flowers in a relatively short period of time.

Masdevallia (maz-de-VAH-lee-a), **'Copperwing'**, Easy to Slightly Difficult. ◑

Temperature: I to C

Color: Copper

Characteristics: Masdevallias are usually partial to cooler temperatures. They are native to the cloud forests high in the Peruvian Andes, a habitat where the entire plant is engulfed in moisture. Masdevallias are distinguished by their lower sepals, which are partially joined at the base and elongate to tail-like tips. In some species the flowers look almost like tiny kites. Most Masdevallia flowers have tubular or triangular shapes; *M.* 'Copperwing' is triangular and quite beautiful. Although many Masdevallias require cool summer temperatures to survive, *M.* 'Copperwing' and other hybrids have been developed specifically with increased tolerance to warmth. I suggest you try this and other varieties termed "intermediate" or "warm growers." These delightful orchids form specimen-size plants readily and bloom in two- and three-inch pots.

Cultural Information: As they don't have pseudobulbs to retain water, Masdevallias should be potted in a medium that holds water and is very fast draining. However, it should be noted they can't stand excess water on their leaves, blossoms or roots because they will rot.

For this reason, it's vital to give Masdevallias excellent air circulation by means of fans.

Miltonia (mil-TONE-ee-a) **Hurricane Ridge 'Sylvia'**, Easy. ◑

Temperature: C to I

Colors: Deep rose with black and white

Characteristics: Miltonia Hurricane Ridge 'Sylvia' is a Colombian-type Miltonia, oftentimes referred to as the "pansy orchid" for its open-faced, flat flowers that are similar to pansies in their shape and markings. Miltonias are epiphytic orchids that have large, graceful leaves and long pseudobulbs. A mature Miltonia in full bloom is quite a sight to behold. The foliage alone can be more than 12 inches across, and the vibrantly colored flowers make an exquisite display.

Cultural Information: There is a distinct difference in the cultural requirements of Colombian and Brazilian Miltonias (for Brazilian Miltonias, please see *Miltonia spectabilis* var. *moreliana*). However, all Miltonias need cool night temperatures (55° to 60° F.) to flower. Daytime temperatures should not exceed 80° F., if possible. Miltonias like to be kept moist, but during the drearier gray days of winter, water them less to decrease the chance of rotting. Miltonias also like high humidity. Like Cymbidiums, Miltonias flower best when pot-bound. Repot them approximately every two years so they can achieve their most impressive size.

These beautiful flowers appear in between the dark green foliage and bloom reliably every year. Miltonia Hurricane Ridge 'Sylvia' is a great Columbian Miltonia for the beginner.

Miltonia spectabilis var. *moreliana,* Easy. ◐ ○

Temperature: I
Color: Purple
Characteristics: One of the finest of all Brazilian Miltonias, *M. spectabilis* var. *moreliana* is a beautiful orchid and one that is exceptionally good for the beginning orchid grower because of its ease of flowering and its ability to grow and bloom on a windowsill. Unlike its Colombian cousin, *Miltonia* Hurricane Ridge 'Sylvia' (see page 60), the Brazilian Miltonia grows in warm conditions similar to those preferred by Cattleyas and Laelias. In appearance, Brazilian Miltonia flowers look nothing like the Colombian variety. Rather than resembling panies, *Miltonia spectabilis* var. *moreliana* and other Brazilian Miltonias look more like Odontoglossums. *Miltonia spectabilis* var. *moreliana* produces large, beautiful purple flowers with a dark purple dorsal, petals and sepals, and a lighter purple lip striped with darker purple. This Miltonia is a rambling type of orchid, and its rhizomes quickly grow over the side of the pot, which tends to make the plant look a little unruly. But the beauty and profusion of the flowers make you forget the somewhat untidy appearance. This plant usually blooms in late summer through early fall.
Cultural Information: Miltonias grow best in fine-textured bark or an epiphytic mix as their roots are relatively delicate. Keep the plant somewhat pot-bound for best flowering. Ensure good air circulation.

Here's a close-up of Miltonia spectabilis *var.* moreliana *mentioned previously. This photo shows the flower shape and coloration of a Brazilian Miltonia.*

Oncidium (on-SID-ee-um) **Golden Sunset 'Brilliant',** Easy. ◐ ○

Temperature: I
Color: Gold with red lip
Characteristics: Oncidiums (or "dancing ladies," as they are commonly called) are wonderful for the beginning orchid grower. If you can provide them with the culture they require, you will be rewarded with spikes of flowers that open successively for many months of bloom. Approximately 500 species make up the genus *Oncidium.* The colors of Oncidiums found in nature are predominantly yellow and brown, yet some are green, white, pink and purple; today's hybrids add shades of orange and red as well. What distinguishes *Oncidium* species is the appearance of a protuberance on the

Here's a close-up of Oncidium Golden Sunset 'Brilliant'. When viewed this closely, the heavily spotted lip is easily detected. When viewed from a distance, the lip appears almost solid. It is a strikingly beautiful Oncidium that is good for beginners.

lip of each flower. These are epiphytic plants and Oncidiums are excellent for windowsill culture and for growing under lights. *O.* Golden Sun 'Brilliant' features all the best qualities sought by Oncidium hybridizers. It has large, full, brilliantly colored flowers, each with a contrasting lip, that appear in great profusion.

Cultural Information: Some Oncidiums have pencil-like leaves, and some have pseudobulbs; all require thorough watering during the growing period and a dry period following new growth. As with most medium to large Oncidiums, use an epiphytic mixture for potting. Small Oncidium varieties can be mounted.

Oncidium papilio, Easy to Slightly Difficult. ○

Temperature: I
Color: Yellow with rust
Characteristics: This Oncidium species is one of the most beautiful. It is an easy orchid

This photograph of my Oncidium papilio *shows the habit of this wonderful Oncidium species, whose name means "butterfly orchid." Taking note of the very elongated stems and the appearance of the flowers on the inflorescence, it's easy to see how this plant got its name.*

A very easy orchid for the beginner is Paphiopedilum bellatum. *As you can see, it is a short-growing orchid with beautifully mottled foliage and highly spotted flowers.*

for the beginner, and you might find it in bloom at any time of the year. *Oncidium papilio* is often referred to as the "butterfly orchid" for its strong resemblance to a butterfly. The flower is yellow and rust on the lip with stripes of chestnut on the petals and sports what looks like three antennae where the dorsal petal ordinarily would be. The flower sits at the very end of a long, thin stem and, swaying in a breeze, seems to float just like a butterfly. The flowers bloom successively, so your *O. papilio* might be in bloom for several months. This orchid species is an easy plant to grow, somewhat more difficult to bloom.

Cultural Information: Don't cut down the stem of *Oncidium papilio* after it flowers, as it blooms repeatedly from the same flower stem. It does best when grown mounted and hung from the ceiling of your greenhouse, where it receives the extra amount of light it needs to bloom.

Paphiopedilum bellatulum (paf-ee-o-PED-i-lum), Easy. ◐

Temperature: I
Colors: Shades of white with red to maroon spots
Characteristics: This beautiful species, native to both Thailand and Burma, prefers growing in intermediate to warm conditions and generally blooms in the spring. *Paphiopedilum bellatulum* has large, broad, fleshy leaves that are prominently mottled. Because the flower stem is very short, particularly for a Paphiopedilum, it often appears that the flower is nestled amid the foliage. Each flower is about two and a half inches across, with drooping petals of white or ivory with maroon or burgundy spots. Some of the most modern varieties have spots nearer to a true red color. *P. bellatulum* is a species easily brought to flower, whether on a windowsill, under lights or in a greenhouse. This species is fairly easily obtained from reputable

orchid dealers and is a good plant for a beginning orchid grower.

Cultural Information: Grow this orchid in intermediate light, in a moisture-retentive mixture; I use New Zealand sphagnum moss. Never let the potting medium go dry. Avoid dividing the plant until it fills its pot and there seems to be no more room.

Paphiopedilum delenatii, Slightly Difficult. ◑ ○

Temperature: I

Color: Soft rose

Characteristics: This is one of the most beautiful Paphiopedilums to be cultivated. It is an intermediate grower, and generally blooms in the summer. *Paphiopedilum delenatii* comes from China and Vietnam. It has beautiful, dark green, mottled foliage. Although it is not as easy to flower as *P. bellatulum*, when it does flower, the blossoms are unforgettable. The flowers, usually two or three at a time, appear on a stem approximately 7 to 8 inches long. Soft rose in color, they are about 3 inches across. *P. delenatii* is somewhat difficult to flower.

Cultural Information: This orchid can be grown under lights, on a windowsill or in a greenhouse. Some growers feel this species needs chilling to flower, that is, dropping the temperature in the area the plant grows. If the orchid is in a basement, under lights or on a windowsill, a window can be opened slightly. Greenhouse owners can lower the temperature by 10° to 15° F. for a two-week period. Some feel this

Paphiopedilum needs high light, and others, intermediate. Experiment to see which works best for you.

Paphiopedilum Francisco Frere, Easy. ● ◑

Temperature: I

Color: Pale rose with yellow

Characteristics: *Paphiopedilum* Francisco Frere is beautiful, producing wonderfully shaped, exquisitely colored flowers. Like other Paphiopedilums, this plant is easy to grow and bloom. And, like other *Paphiopedilum* hybrids, this one provides long-lasting flowers. When mature, the plant is covered with blooms. The foliage is light green and mottled. I strongly recommend *P. Francisco Frere* for its beauty and ease of blooming.

Cultural Information: This *Paphiopedilum* will thrive and bloom under lights, on a windowsill and in a greenhouse. As is the case with other mottled-foliage Paphiopedilums, it prefers warmer temperatures than do the solid-green-leaved Paphiopedilums. Paphiopedilums can be grown in either plastic or clay pots. I prefer plastic because it retains water longer, which benefits the roots.

My Paphiopedilum Francisco Frere generally blooms two times a year, and the flowers are softly colored with a pinkish green lip and a delicately spotted, yellowish green flower.

Somewhat more difficult to flower, Paphiopedilum delenatii *is a species well worth trying. The soft pink pouch and white sepals and petals present themselves on tall spikes.*

This orchid seems to be glowing from within. When viewing this orchid up close, it is darker in appearance than this photograph shows. It is truly a spectacular vinicolor.

No orchid grower should be without Paphiopedilum malipoense. *Just look at the beautiful green flower, the white full lips, slight striations—all presented on long stately stems. To complete the picture in this Paphiopedilum species, the flowers smell like fresh raspberries.*

Paphiopedilum Macabre 'Black Lace,' Easy. ● ◐

Temperature: I

Color: Deepest purple

Characteristics: This type of *Paphiopedilum*, referred to as a vinicolor because of its dark wine red color, represents one of the newest trends in *Paphiopedilum* breeding. Judges present their awards based on the darkness of the flower (as well as the size, length and strength of flower stem, and so on), and the darker the flower, the better. Like all *Paphiopedilum* hybrids, Macabre 'Black Lace' is a beautiful orchid that is easy to grow and bloom.

Cultural Information: Cultural requirements do not differ from those of other Paphiopedilums discussed in this book; refer to *Paphiopedilum* Francisco Frere (page 63) for information.

Paphiopedilum malipoense, Easy to Slightly Difficult. ◐ ○

Temperature: I

Color: Green

Characteristics: Paphiopedilum malipoense has to be one of the most incredible acquisitions for the beginner. It is one of the only five Paphiopedilum species native to China and Vietnam. The foliage is dark green and mottled, leaves larger than those of other Chinese Paphiopedilums. But the dramatic foliage is secondary to the flower. *P. malipoense* produces a huge, green flower with a large pouch (the lip in Paphiopedilums forms a pouch) and a fragrance like fresh raspberries. Imagine the amazement at seeing this plant bloom for the first time! First you can detect signs of a spike forming. Each day the bud increases in size, and the stem lengthens a bit. Several weeks later, finally at 10 to 12 inches, the bud begins to open on your *P. malipoense,* and you realize the wait was worth it. It is not the easiest orchid to flower, but the chances are very good that with the proper culture it will bloom for you. Then, you'll surely want to add ten or twenty more *P. malipoense* to your collection.

Cultural Information: I grow one of my *Paphiopedilum malipoense* in New Zealand sphagnum moss and two more in a coarse bark mixture. All are planted in plastic pots, and they seem to thrive and bloom equally well.

Paphiopedilum micranthum, Slightly Difficult. ◐ ○

Temperature: I

Color: Bubble-gum pink

Characteristics: This is one of the most unusual of the Chinese Paphiopedilums. Despite its name "*micranthum*"—which literally means "little flower"—*P. micranthum* has one of the largest flowers of all the Chinese Paphiopediums. The huge, bubble-gum pink pouch is what makes the plant so striking. Flowering generally occurs in fall or winter. The foliage is very dark green and mottled. When viewing *P. micranthum* at orchid shows or at show tables, it is easy to become confused, as some *P. micranthums* often look much larger than others. This is because some varieties are tetraploid and produce much larger flowers. The plant never grows tall; it simply sends out more and more "fans," groups of leaves. However, it can flower on just one fan.

Cultural Information: Given the proper culture, this orchid can flower when small. New growth appears from underground rhizomes. Like all Chinese Paphiopedilums, *P. micranthum* prefers warm night temperatures, moderate to abundant watering and moderate light. All the Chinese Paphiopedilums I mentioned in the Orchid Portraits will tolerate somewhat cooler night temperatures.

Paphiopedilum Vanda M. Pearman, Easy. ◑

Temperature: I

Colors: Soft pink, white

Characteristics: If you admire the beautiful spotting and round shape of *Paphiopedilum bellatulum* and the soft pink color and longer flower stem of *P. delenatii*, then you will want to acquire *P.* Vanda M. Pearman, a fairly recent cross made between these two Paphiopedilums. *P.* Vanda M. Pearman has very dark, mottled foliage and is an intermediate grower. It generally blooms in winter. The three-inch flowers, which are either white or a very soft pink in color, have delicate crimson spotting. What is interesting is that the spotting is

Here's another one of my personal favorites. Another Chinese Paphiopedilum species, like malipoense and delenatii, Paphiopedilum micranthum *is commonly referred to as the bubble gum orchid. You can see why. It can be difficult to flower, but when it does it's well worth the wait.*

Paphiopedilum Vanda S. Pearman is a hybrid that blooms on my windowsill and under lights three times a year. It's a wonderful orchid for the beginner to try.

heavier on the pouch of the flower than on the petals, unusual for light-colored Paphiopedilums. *P.* Vanda M. Pearman is a wonderful plant for a beginner. It is easily flowered on a windowsill, under lights or in a greenhouse. Given good culture, it often blooms more than once a year.

Cultural Information: Same as for *Paphiopedilum* Francisco Frere (page 63).

Phalaenopsis Hilo Lip is a relatively new introduction in Phalaenopsis breeding. The white lip against the deep rose-colored lip makes this orchid very beautiful.

Another relatively recent trend in Phalaenopsis hybridizing is toward yellow Phalaenopsis.

Phalaenopsis (FAL-a-nop-sis), **Hilo Lip '#1'**, Easy. ● ◑
Temperature: I to W
Color: Dark pink with white
Characteristics: *Phalaenopsis* Hilo Lip '#1' is an exceptionally striking orchid with a beautiful dark pink flower. What sets this plant apart is the stark white lip, which is an outstanding contrast. The finest specimens of Hilo Lip have a very deep pink color and a pure white lip. *P.* Hilo Lip is typical of one of the newer trends in *Phalaenopsis* breeding, a move away from the traditional white petals and sepals with a reddish lip. This is a striking and worthwhile orchid for the beginning grower. It should be relatively easy to locate for purchase from orchid growers (see page 90).
Cultural Information: Like other *Phalaenopsis*, Hilo Lip '#1' needs to be kept warm and placed in an area that receives indirect light. Make sure that water doesn't remain in the crown of the plant after watering.

Phalaenopsis schilleriana, Easy. ● ◑
Temperature: I to W
Color: Purple-rose
Characteristics: This is one of the most famous of all *Phalaenopsis* species, noted for its magnificent leaves more than any other feature. It grows under warm conditions and generally blooms in the springtime. *P. schilleriana* comes from Manilla, where it was sighted growing in the tops of trees; the plants attach themselves to tree branches by means of flattened roots. When

The leaves of Phalaenopsis schilleriana *are even more outstanding than the flowers to some orchid lovers.*

This star-shaped flower, white tinged with green and the raspberry coloration, just complements the incredible green glossy leaves of Phalaenopsis violacea *var. Borneo.*

P. schilleriana is cultivated, the roots grow very long and are extremely tenacious. As a matter of fact, it is almost impossible to remove a *P. schilleriana* root once it has implanted itself on a mount or the side of a pot without breaking it. This decorative species has 18-inch-or-longer leaves that are considered even more beautiful than the flowers; they are dark green and marbled with variations of gray and silver. In bloom the plant is unbeatable, with soft purplish rose flowers, three inches across, that appear in great profusion on a long spike. This is a great plant for the beginning orchidist, as it blooms quite easily and is beautiful both in and out of flower.

Cultural Information: Phalaenopsis schilleriana is exceptionally hardy and will grow and bloom under lights, on a south windowsill or in a greenhouse. One point to remember: It likes warmth.

Phalaenopsis violacea var. *borneo,* Slightly Difficult. ◑ ○

Temperature: W

Colors: Green and cream with blue-violet or purple-rose

Characteristics: Phalaenopsis violacea, while not an easy plant for the beginning orchidist to grow, is one of the most beautiful of the *Phalaenopsis* species. It's fragrant and well worth trying if you can obtain the plant at a reasonable price. I suggest you buy an established plant of substantive size—a plant that has bloomed previously and has a leaf span of 6 to 8 inches—rather than a seedling plant. *P. violacea* is native to Malaysia and Borneo. As is the case with all orchids, its geographical distribution in the wild describes the type of culture it prefers in your home. The Malaysian and the Bornean types of *P. violacea* differ in appearance. The larger Bornean flowers smell like violets. The fragrant Malaysian varieties are smaller and fuller. The flowers of *P. violacea* are green or cream and have either blue-violet or deeper purple-rose markings on the petals and lip. The top petals and sepals are generally green and white, and the lower part of the flower purplish in color. The flower color may vary considerably; some flowers are deep green, and a vibrant purple suffuses the lower lip. The flowers are borne on somewhat thick inflorescences 4 to 6 inches long. One of the benefits of this beautiful species is that the flowers open successively over a long period—several months, sometimes three or four. It is not

Can you believe the incredible color of the Phragmipedium besseae *'Eat My Dust'? It's hard to believe that this species of Phragmipedium went unnoticed in the wild until recently.*

Another wonderful Phragmipedium with the exceptionally long petals is my own plant of Phragmipedium grande. *Although not shown in this photograph, there were over 10 flowers in bloom at one time.*

uncommon to have two or three flowers open at one time. Often as they begin to fade, a fresh one is beginning to open.

Cultural Information: This species likes a warm, moderately shaded location with high humidity. You might want to try this plant under lights, but position it on the lower shelves where it can be shaded by the leaves of another plant. When you water the plant, don't allow water to collect in the crown of the plant. If this happens, the orchid will suffer crown rot and you will lose it. I offer two tips for success with Phalaenopsis: First, gently wipe the center of the plant with a tissue after watering. Second, follow the example of one outstanding grower of Phalaenopsis, Marilyn Mirro, of Long Island, New York, who grows her *P. violacea* in slatted baskets and hangs them on a slant, so water naturally drains out of the center.

Phragmipedium besseae (FRAG-mi-pee-de-um), 'Eat My Dust', Easy to Slightly Difficult. ◐ ○

Temperature: I

Colors: Bright red, orange-red; variable

Characteristics: Phragmipedium besseae, a strikingly beautiful plant, is a relatively newly discovered *Phragmipedium* species. Orchid growers wonder how this vibrantly colored *Phragmipedium* could have remained undiscovered in the wild for so long. Although variable in color, *P. besseae* is generally bright red or orangish red in color. This small-flowered orchid is native to

both Ecuador and Peru. The leaves are dark green, and the inflorescence bears from one to six flowers that appear in succession. A *P. besseae* from Peru looks quite different from the species from Ecuador. The Peruvian variety has wider petals and a much rounder, fuller flower than the Ecuadorian type. Conversely, *P. besseae* from Ecuador has a pointier, more star-shaped flower. If you can obtain this orchid at a price you can afford, by all means get it. It is not a fussy plant, will tolerate overwatering (often inflicted by beginners on their orchids) and offers the most beautiful blooms.

Cultural Information: Like all Phragmipediums, which are terrestrial orchids, *P. besseae* likes to be potted in a mixture that is kept moist all the time. As a matter of fact, some orchid growers grow their Phragmipediums in water-filled saucers during the summer months.

Phragmipedium grande, Easy. ◐ ○

Temperature: I

Colors: Tan, green and dark burgundy

Characteristics: Phragmipedium grande is more typical of the genus in coloring and overall appearance than *P. besseae.* Many Phragmipediums have greenish, tan, brown, pink or rose coloration. They are noted for petals that may be twisted or straight, and are often quite long; if the orchid is set on a greenhouse bench and given plenty of room, the leaves may touch the floor. *P. grande* is an attractive plant with many long, straplike leaves and large, dark maroon, pouched flowers that open successively; the long petals, left unhindered, will grow very long. I recommend that every beginner try his or her hand at growing *P. grande*. Although Phragmipediums in general are not easy to find at nurseries or orchid plant sales, in most areas of the country *P. grande* is more readily available than *P. besseae*, and at a more reasonable price. Try to find another orchid grower in your area who has a large plant of *P. grande*, perhaps he or she would be willing to sell you a division.

Cultural Information: Leave this orchid potbound for better flowering. It likes a moist medium.

Sarcochilus (sar-ko-KI-lus)

hartmanii × **Pinky**, Easy. ◐ ○
Temperature: I
Colors: White, shades of pink
Characteristics: Sarcochilus are not among the best-known orchids and this is unfortunate because they are delightful and easy to grow (particularly nice for the new orchid grower). There are about 14 known species of these dwarf monopodial epiphytes. Some come from Asia, and others from Australia. *S. hartmanii,* one of the parents in the cross *Sarcochilus hartmanii* × Pinky, is native to Australia and well known among orchid growers for its floriferous habit and easy cultivation. Although the flowers are dainty and delicate, the plants are long-lived and will grow into incredibly showy specimens in a relatively short period—within a few years, if

given good culture. This genus generally flowers in spring. Some species are fragrant.

Cultural Information: Sarcochilus hartmanii × Pinky grows best in shallow pots with a coarse potting material for the growing medium. For those of you who prefer having some of your plants mounted, you can grow *Sarcochilus* on a tree fern slab. It will do well under lights and on a sunny windowsill.

Slc. **Carol Ann** × *Laelia sincorana,* Easy. ◐ ○

Temperature: I
Color: Deep pink
Characteristics: Here is a delightful, wonderful plant for the beginning orchid grower. The flower is exquisite, and the plant blooms very easily and is extremely compact—excellent for growing on a windowsill or under lights, and small enough so there is room for more than one. Laelias are very closely related to Cattleyas, and this is readily seen if plants of each are placed side by side. For the most part, though, the petals of Laelias are narrower than Cattleya petals. Laelias are epiphytic plants, which should be grown in pots. They will do wonderfully for you if grown in an east- or south-facing window or under lights. As a beginning orchid grower, you might want to try other Laelia crosses as they, too, will be relatively easy to grow and bloom. Please note that rupiculous Laelias are more difficult to flower since they require a great deal of light; in nature, they grow in rocky localities.

Sarcochilus hartmannii × *Pinky clearly displays some of the most delicate colors, yet striking appearance, of the genus. Each bud will open sequentially, keeping this small growing plant in bloom for a long time.*

This photograph accurately shows the plant habit and flower size of Slc. Carol Ann × *Laelia sincorana. The plant is growing in a 3-inch plastic pot, and the beautiful deep rose flower is quite large. This is typical of many miniature Cattleyas.*

Cultural Information: Suitable potting mixes include osmunda and fir bark. When grown in relatively small pots, these plants will bloom more abundantly. As Laelias (like Cattleyas) like house temperatures, your windowsill is the perfect spot for this plant. Hybrid Laelias like to be watered thoroughly and then allowed to dry out. After your Laelia has flowered, let it rest and decrease the water somewhat until new roots and a new growth appear; then, resume normal watering.

Slc. **Regal Gold** 'Laina', Easy. ◐

Temperature: I to W
Color: Yellow and red, often with orange.
Characteristics: Sophrolaeliacattleya Regal Gold 'Laina' is one of the finest miniature Cattleyas for the beginning orchid

Beautiful, highly colored flowers in shades of yellow, red and orange adorn this miniature Cattleya, Slc. Regal Gold 'Laina'. This orchid grows on my windowsill and blooms reliably two, sometimes three, times a year.

grower to try. It blooms quite readily on a south- or east-facing windowsill, and can be made to bloom under lights with ease. Obviously, this orchid would be 'a natural' in a greenhouse. Although the flowers are not as spectacular as those of the larger Cattleya types, they are very beautiful in their own right, and the plant is so prolific it will give you much joy. It blooms several times a year. The plant generally grows no more than eight inches high, with many pseudobulbs, each producing two or three small, yellow flowers tipped in orange or red. The tiny lip of the flower is generally deep red. When the plant is covered with flowers, it is quite impressive.
Cultural Information: This orchid hybrid is very easy to grow and bloom. Try it on your windowsill, under lights or in your greenhouse. Intermediate conditions as to light and temperature are best; it likes warmth.

Slc. Virgin Queen is another wonderful small-size Cattleya. Although larger than a miniature, it is not overly large and it provides the grower with these wonderful, pure white flowers, usually three at a time, at least twice a year. This is my plant, and I can easily tell when it's in bloom by the wonderful fragrance.

Slc. **Virgin Queen,** Easy. ◐

Temperature: I
Color: White
Characteristics: This is one of the most beautiful of the Cattleyatype orchids, producing large, white, exceptionally fragrant flowers on a relatively small plant, some 8 to 12 inches tall. In bloom, this plant is covered with a profusion of white flowers, the type typically seen in women's corsages. I have grown this plant from seedlings and am always thrilled when it comes into bloom for its crystalline whiteness and the large size of the flowers on such a relatively small plant. On a windowsill or under lights, this orchid bloom will fill the room with a deliciously sweet aroma. This is an exceptionally beautiful and easy plant for the beginning orchid grower.
Cultural Information: I grow this orchid in New Zealand

sphagnum moss, in a 4-inch slotted clay pot (commonly called an azalea pot), and let it become potbound before repotting it. Growing this plant on a windowsill might be preferable to growing it under lights, as it is easier to get lower temperatures near a window than under lights; the plant does like a bit of coolness.

Vanda (VAN-dah) **Snow Angel,** Slightly Difficult. ○
Temperature: W
Colors: White
Characteristics: You will note there are not many Vandas listed in these Orchid Portraits. Generally speaking, Vandas are not the easiest of plants for the beginner; they need a high level of light, high humidity and excellent air circulation, and they take up lots of room. They are obviously not "under-lights" plants. However, no one remains a beginning orchid grower forever, and as Vanda flowers are exquisite, so large and vibrantly colored, you might want to expend the extra effort needed to grow them. (If you're sure you *cannot* provide the correct culture for them, you might opt for the vibrantly colored Ascocendas. They are smaller and can be grown under lights. Growth habit is monopodial, and these orchids are grown in baskets so that their roots are free to hang loosely and to absorb whatever moisture is present in the air.
Cultural Information: There are orchid growers who don't have a greenhouse, and yet they grow Vandas with success. They have equipped their homes— usually their basements—with

metal halide lights, heaters and many fans to duplicate the conditions Vandas thrive in naturally. As Vandas are found in such tropical areas as Indonesia, the Philippines and Malaysia, it is no surprise that they need high temperatures to survive; orchid nurseries in the Philippines, Florida and Hawaii are renowned for their Vandas. Still, if the determination and motivation for growing these exquisite orchids is great enough, they can be grown beautifully even in the Northeast. One of the finest Vanda growers in the United States, Marilyn Mirro, lives on Long Island, New York, and because she provides her Vandas with the conditions they love, they thrive. The roots are very tenacious, and it is not advisable to try to remove a Vanda from the basket it is growing in; simply place it, basket and all, into a larger basket. (Ascocendas should be "repotted" in the same way.)

Zygopetalum (zye-go-PET-a-lum) **'Artur Elle',** Easy. ◐ ○
Temperature: I to C
Color: Green with dark brown stripes and white lip striped with purple
Characteristics: Orchids of the genus *Zygopetalum* should be a part of every orchid grower's collection. Not only are the flowers beautiful in appearance, but the fragrance of most Zygopetalums is also incredible and unforgettable. Set your flowering *Zygopetalum* in a room you and your family frequent often, and a most beautiful, sweet scent will fill the air. Another attribute is that the flowers are exceptionally long-

lasting. *Zygopetalum* 'Artur Elle' is compact in growth, beautifully colored and floriferous. Zygopetalums have large, glossy leaves that are sometimes deciduous when the plant is mature. Most are native to Brazil.
Cultural Information: Unlike many orchids, Zygopetalums are terrestrial orchids that need a very well-draining potting medium. Never mist Zygopetalums because the foliage is easily spotted by water.

For lovers of white flowers, Vanda Snow Angel will give you wonderfully large, white flowers if you can provide the cultural requirements of high humidity, good air movement and high temperatures.

This is my Zygopetalum Artur Elle. This plant perfumes the entire room with its lilac-like fragrance. Additionally, this plant has wonderful coloration. Notice the brown barring on the green leaves and the white lip heavily veined in magenta-to-purple colors.

PESTS AND DISEASES

Orchids are very hardy plants with a strong determination to survive. Nevertheless, they are subject to the problems of pests and diseases. If you use a clean, airy location to grow your orchids and provide the right amount of humidity and ventilation, you will certainly decrease the likelihood of pest or disease infestation.

Even in the best of situations, pests may attack your plants. As an orchid grower you must be constantly watchful for any change in the appearance of your plants. Diligence in surveying your growing area and in taking control of a pest or disease problem before it gets control of your plants is the best approach. The most successful orchid growers are those individuals who vigilantly oversee the growth and performance of their plants. To paraphrase an old adage that is particularly applicable to orchid growing, "An ounce of prevention is worth a pound of cure." To help thwart the development of pest colonies, remove any withered flower, leaf or bract from your orchids so insects are not given the chance to hide in the dried bloom or foliage and multiply.

If, despite your best efforts, you notice a problem with your plants, look below for assistance. There are numerous pesticides available in dry powder and liquid forms, both of which are diluted with water before use. The two types are equally effective and will easily control your pests if the manufacturer's directions are followed.

Please note that the strength of insecticide is just as deadly in the dry form as in the liquid form. Caution must be taken to protect the user from the dust of the powders as well as the fumes of the liquid type. When preparing and applying a pesticide, it is advisable to wear a face mask and make only the amount you plan to use immediately. Most recently introduced insecticides are readily biodegradable and will break down within 24 hours to 10 days, depending on the insecticide used.

PRIMARY PESTS AFFLICTING ORCHIDS

If you are unsure of the type of insect affecting your orchid plant, an examination of the symptoms should provide you with the correct identification. While commercial insecticides can cure your orchid's pest problem, insecticides are not preventative and should be used only when you actually see pests on your plants.

APHIDS ARE PROBABLY THE CULPRITS IF:

♦ the insects are clustered in the soft parts of the plant, particularly around the tips of new shoots
♦ they exude a sticky material, which becomes black and sooty in appearance

- the flowers fail to open or appear malformed
- the leaves and the stems are stunted
- the orchids most often preyed on by aphids are *Cattleya, Phalaenopsis* and *Oncidium*

Solution: Wash off any black "soot" with water and mild kitchen detergent. Use an insecticide containing a systemic poison, such as acephate (Orthene), Diazinon or malathion. You can easily identify the insect on new growth.

MEALY BUGS ARE THE PROBLEM IF:

- orchid plants appear shriveled or stunted
- you see a cottonlike mass on your plants, particularly in the crooks (joints) between the leaves and stems or on the undersides of leaves and buds
- the orchids most susceptible are *Cattleya, Phalaenopsis* and *Dendrobium* (although other orchid genera) can be affected as well)

Solution: If the infestation is not severe, you can remove the mealy bugs by applying rubbing alcohol to a cotton swab and dabbing the offending bugs. If the problem really is severe, use Orthene, carbaryl, Diazinon or malathion, following the manufacturer's directions carefully.

SCALE IS PROBABLY INFECTING YOUR PLANTS IF:

- you see round or oval shells in white, brown or gray on your plant, particularly on the undersides of the leaves or on the pseudobulbs of Cattleyas
- the plant appears stunted
- the leaves are turning yellow and falling off
- there are pale spots on the leaves
- the orchids most susceptible are *Paphiopedilum, Cymbidium* and *Cattleya*

Solution: A small infestation of scale can be removed with tweezers or with swabs wetted with rubbing alcohol. If your scale problems are bad, you can use the same treatment as you'd use for mealy bugs or aphids—Orthene, Diazinon or malathion.

SLUGS, SNAILS AND CATERPILLARS ARE MOST LIKELY YOUR PROBLEM IF:

- you see that the leaves of your plants have irregularly shaped holes and tears
- large portions of a leaf are

missing, or only the veins of the leaf remain
- you can see a slimy trail, which reveals the route the slug or snail has traveled
- most of the damage appears to be occurring at night
- your orchid seedlings are particularly affected

Solution: If you see a slug or snail near your orchids, simply putting a chunk of wood near the stems will almost certainly protect the flowers; slugs usually avoid wood. The most effective chemical treatment against slugs, snails and caterpillars is metaldehyde. In powder form it can be sprinkled on

the affected plants; as a liquid, it should be watered in. Another means of dealing with these pests (certainly less than scientific, but effective) is to lure them into little saucers of beer, where they drown.

RED SPIDER MITES AND FALSE SPIDER MITES ARE THE CULPRITS IF:

♦ the leaves and stems of your plant are stippled white or gray

♦ there is a white, webbed look on the undersides of the leaves
♦ the orchids most susceptible are *Dendrobium*, *Catasetum*, *Cymbidium* and *Lycaste*.

Solution: To rid your plants of red spider mites or false spider mites, rinse the foliage thoroughly with tepid water; you may need to rub gently. This will break up the webs. If there's a heavy infestation, use a pesticide such as chlorobenzilate.

BACTERIAL AND FUNGAL DISEASES

Bacteria and fungi generally affect plants in a weakened condition. Even if your plants are robust, to ensure a minimum amount of fungal and bacterial problems, make certain that your growing environment is kept clean. Plants that are watered too frequently, that endure excessive humidity or that are left wet when the temperature drops are prime candidates for problems, both fungal and bacterial. It's imperative for orchids grown together to have good air circulation. This is true for most plants, but particularly applicable to orchids. The surest way to encourage problems—fungus and rot, spotting and root rot—is to allow your plants to sit in a humid atmosphere without fans to move the air around. Good air movement is so important to the health of orchids that many commercial growers, as well as hobbyists, consider the proper use of fans and cooling devices the most important factor in growing fine quality, healthy orchids. If you are fortunate enough to have a greenhouse in which to grow your orchids, you should regularly remove any weeds; they can harbor disease and pests.

BLACK ROT FUNGUS MAY BE PRESENT IF:

♦ you see soft, rotted areas on the leaves or in new rhizomes (which go on to spread down into the roots)
♦ the soft spots initially are purplish brown and later turn black

Solution: Use a fungicide such as Truban or Banort. Make sure you remove all of the infected spots; cut into healthy tissue by about 1 inch and then seal off the infected area with fungicide. Be sure to sterilize the scissors or knife in a flame between cuts. If an orchid is badly infected with black rot, throw it away.

LEAF SPOT MAY BE PRESENT IF:

♦ the leaves have purplish brown or black sunken spots
♦ yellowish spots appear on the undersides of the leaves
♦ a darkening of the spots on both sides of the leaves appear (a classic symptom)

Solution: Problems with leaf spot can be avoided by improving the air circulation and decreasing the humidity. Remove infected leaves. Spray the remaining leaves with a fungicide such as Benlate or another containing benomyl every week until the problem is gone.

PETAL BLIGHT MAY BE PRESENT IF:

♦ black or brown spots with pinkish margins appear on the petals
♦ *Cattleya* and spring-blooming *Phalaenopsis*, in particular, are affected

Solution: Cut off the infected flowers and destroy them. Use a fungicide such as Benlate or one containing benomyl, zineb or ferbam on the plants.

ROOT ROT FUNGUS MAY BE PRESENT IF:

♦ the orchid plant has wilted
♦ the rhizomes become soft and brown
♦ the leaves are twisted and yellow in appearance

Solution: Repot the orchid as soon as the problem is suspected. Use fresh potting material and a sterile pot. Cut off all the diseased spots using a knife sterilized between each cut. Take the plant outdoors and spray it with a fungicide such as Benlate 'or one containing benomyl.

BACTERIAL BROWN SPOT MAY BE PRESENT IF:

♦ the spots on the leaves are sunken, appear water soaked and turn brown to black
♦ when the spots are touched, they exude a brownish liquid

Solution: First remove all infected leaves. Bring your plant to an outdoor area and spray it with RD 20. Make sure that you isolate this plant from others, as the liquid exudate from the infected plant can spread the disease to other orchids.

Hints for Growing Pest- and Disease-Free Orchids

To keep the good health of your plants and to maintain them as pest- and disease-free as possible, check the plants you purchase or receive as gifts for visible pests. Be sure the leaves and flowers do not exhibit signs of fungal or bacterial disease. You can help protect your plants by providing adequate air circulation and the right amount of humidity. Avoid wet foliage when the temperature drops.

Note: The use of poisons in your home must be carefully controlled. If your plants grow where you live, you should be extra careful. Prior to using malathion, sevin (carbaryl), or another insecticide on your orchids, isolate the plants for treatment in an area where there is adequate ventilation.

VIRUSES

The most dreaded word to orchid growers is "virus." Beginning orchid growers look at every marked leaf or malformed flower and immediately think, "Oh no, my plant is infected with a virus and now all of my other plants will become infected as well!" Many other problems that affect orchids are mistaken for virus, so it is important to recognize the distinctions.

YOUR PLANT PROBABLY IS INFECTED WITH A VIRUS IF:

♦ black, red or yellow streaks appear on the leaves
♦ black, red or yellow spots mar the leaves
♦ the flowers are marred by a mosaic pattern or by white or brown streaking

Solution: If you suspect your plant has a virus, you should have it tested to confirm the diagnosis. Quarantine your plant if you suspect a viral infection. If you know for certain, throw the infected orchid away, rather than risk contaminating your other plants. Plant viruses are incurable. Because plants may be infected without showing symptoms, it's very important that you sterilize your tools after you work on your plants.

ORCHID GROWERS' MOST-ASKED QUESTIONS

Beginning orchid growers have many questions about their orchid plants, and this is to be expected. Even long-time orchid growers appreciate information and culture tips from other "experts." Orchid growing is not an exact science, but rather a cultivated art, so what works for one grower may not work (at least, in quite the same way) for another. We are all familiar with the scenario where one commercial grower states emphatically, "I never use tap water on my orchids," only to be confronted with another successful orchid grower, who says, "Tap water seems to be the best type for my orchids." Why is this example so often cited? Simply because everyone's growing conditions differ. How often do you water? What daytime and evening temperatures do your orchids grow in? How much humidity do your plants get? Do you grow your orchids in fir bark, osmunda, or New Zealand sphagnum moss? Do you grow in clay or plastic pots? As an orchid grower striving to succeed with your hobby, you are encouraged to read all the pertinent material you can find. However, in the final analysis, *you* have to be the judge of what works best for your orchids.

Question: How often should I water my plants?
Answer: As I mentioned in the discussion of orchid culture, this is perhaps the toughest question to answer. Everyone's conditions differ, and you must judge your plants' performance and evaluate your habits and your success rate. Some general rules apply:

♦ When in doubt, don't. More orchids die from overwatering than from any other cause.

♦ Orchids in clay pots generally need watering more often than orchids in plastic pots.

♦ Plants mounted on cork and tree fern and in baskets dry out more quickly and therefore need more water than those that are potted.

♦ Plants bearing pseudobulbs can retain water longer than those without pseudobulbs. Cattleyas and Odontoglossums, for example, are more water retentive than Phalaenopsis and Paphiopedilums, which need more frequent watering.

♦ Orchids potted in fir bark, tree fern or osmunda generally need watering more often than those in New Zealand sphagnum moss, which tends to retain water.

Question: How often should I repot my orchids?
Answer: As a rule, orchids should be repotted when they have outgrown their container. Repotting is also necessary when the potting mix has deteriorated. Inorganic materials last forever, whereas such organic ones as fir bark and osmunda last for about three years—sometimes less, sometimes more. Tree fern slabs and cork slabs last considerably longer, sometimes up to six years. Again, know your plants. If an orchid

doesn't seem to be thriving, or if you see a definite decline, check the roots and look at the potting medium to see if it's still in good condition; if it has disintegrated or seems mushy, repot. Bear in mind that some orchids like to be potbound; let them remain in their pots and you'll see much better flowering.

Question: How can I get my orchid to bloom?
Answer: You may be frustrated because you bought an orchid in bloom, brought it home, enjoyed the lovely flowers and are now waiting for the orchid to bloom again—and it hasn't. To increase the flowering, give the plant higher light, whether on a windowsill, under lights or in a greenhouse. A slight shift of a few inches may make all the difference in whether your orchid blooms or not. Try using a fertilizer such as 10-30-20 formula (a blossom booster) on your orchids, too. This should help induce bloom.

Question: Can I grow different types of orchids if I live in an apartment?
Answer: Your choices for growing in an apartment are diverse. Read The Orchid Growing Guide (page 29) and Orchid Portraits (page 51) to learn about the incredible number of species and hybrid orchids that can thrive in your home. If you're dedicated to your hobby and try to meet the humidity, light and temperature requirements of the orchids you delight in, you will be successful. Some of the orchids you can grow in an apartment include: *Phalaenopsis, Paphiopedilum, Oncidium, Dendrobium, Miltonia, Encyclia* and miniature *Cattleyas.* When embarking on orchid growing, you may find it worthwhile to obtain mature or blooming-size plants rather than seedlings, which can take several years before flowering.

Question: What type of humidity is best for my orchids?
Answer: Most orchids will do well in humidity levels of approximately 50% to 70%. Grouping your plants together, placing them on an egg crate tray over wet pebbles, misting them often (only for those types not adversely affected by this!) and using a humidifier will all help to increase the humidity in your orchid-growing area. This will benefit not only your orchids but you and your family as well.

Please write or call for a free Burpee catalog:

W. Atlee Burpee & Co.
300 Park Avenue
Warminster, PA 18974
(215) 674-9633

GLOSSARY

AERIAL: existing and growing in the air

AGAR: a gelatinlike substance, derived from certain seaweeds, used to solidify culture media; culture media are used for germinating orchid seeds and also in the propagation of plants using meristem culture

ALBA or *ALBINO:* absence of red pigmentation in flowers that are generally white or yellow

ALTERNATE: occurring first on one side and then on another side, as on a stem; not opposite or paired

AM: Award of Merit

ANTERIOR: the surface to the front

ANTHER: the part of the flower stamen that contains the pollen

AOS: American Orchid Society

APETALOUS: without petals

APEX, APICAL: the tip, top or pointed end; relating to the apex

APHYLLOUS: without leaves

ARACHNOID: spiderlike in appearance

ARTICULATE: having joints

ASEXUAL: propagation without sex, i.e., without exchanging male and female cells, as by division or by mericlone

AUXIN: a plant growth hormone

AXIL: upper angle formed with the stem by a leaf or branch

BACKBULB: generally, an old pseudobulb, one without leaves, found behind the actively growing part of a sympodial orchid, such as a Cymbidium; it is made up of living tissue and usually bears one or more buds

BASAL: forming at the base

BICOLOR: having two colors

BIFOLIATE: having two leaves on each new growth, such as the orchid *Cattleya skinneri*

BLC.: refers to the fact that this genus is a combination of *Brassia, Laelia* and *Cattleya*

BOTANICAl: any genus or species of orchids that is not grown commercially for its flowers

CALLUS: a thickening or protuberance on a flower part

CAPSULE: the seed pod

CHLOROTIC: of or relating to a plant condition in which the chlorophyll breaks down; in an orchid, the color is abnormally yellow

CHROMOSOME: one of the rodlike structures in the nuclei of cells that carry the hereditary genes, experienced as characteristics

CLONES: genetically identical plant(s) propagated from one specimen

COLUMN: the central organ of an orchid flower, formed by the male and female parts

COMMUNITY POT: the container ordinarily used by an orchid propagator when a group of seedlings are removed from their flask—a sterile jar where seedlings develop—prior to their being potted individually; the seedlings are all placed in a community pot, generally 10 to 30 seedlings in a fine potting mix.

CONCOLOR: of or relating to an orchid of one color only, generally yellows or whites, sometimes green

CULTIVAR: [combination of *culti*vated and *vari*ety] an original plant or a propagation grown vegetatively, rather than by means of sexual reproduction

DECIDUOUS: of or relating to plants that shed their leaves seasonally

DIVISION: a method of propagating orchids by breaking or cutting away the pseudobulbs or stems

DORSAL: in orchids, the uppermost petal

EPIPHYTE: an orchid that grows on trees or similar supports; it can be potted in bark, tree fern or coarse, nonsoil media, or mounted on a piece of cork or fir bark

EYE: the budding sprout of a vegetative growth, particularly in sympodial orchids

FCC: First Class Certificate, an award of distinction given to orchids receiving 90 points or more in formal judging

GENUS: [plural genera] Botanical nomenclature referring to a subdivision of a family and consisting of one or more subcategories (species) that show similar characteristics and appear to have a common ancestry

GREX: the name of a new orchid formed when two different orchids are crossed; for example, the grex name of the cross of *Paphiopedilum bellatum* with *Paphiopedilum delenatii* is *Paphiopedilum* Vanda M. Pearman

HABIT: the characteristic form of a plant

HABITAT: the place where a plant originated naturally; the conditions in which it thrives in nature

HCC: Highly Commended Certificate, an award given to orchids receiving 75 to 79 points in formal orchid judging

INFLORESCENCE: all the flowers on a common stem

INTERGENERIC: between two or more genera

INTERSPECIFIC: between two or more species

KEIKI: small plantlets that form by asexual propagation on some orchid varieties, particularly Phalaenopsis

LABELLUM: the "lip" of an orchid flower that is actually a modified petal

LEACHING: the process of washing away something, such as mineral salts; often used in conjunction with the fertilization of orchid plants

LEAD: the active growing stem on an orchid, especially one having sympodial, as opposed to monopodial, growths, as on Cattleyas, Laelias and Cymbidiums

LIP: the *labellum*, a modified petal that is usually different from the other orchid petals in color and size

LITHOPHYTE: a plant that grows among rocks and gets its nutrients from the organic matter within range of its roots

MERICLONE: a plant produced by meristem or tissue culture

MERISTEM: plant tissue used to propagate genetically identical plants

MONOPODIAL: having bud growth from a single, central terminal, as with Vanda and Phalaenopsis rather than from pseudobulbs

MUTATION: an individual that is an unexpected departure from the parent type due to a genetic change

NATURAL HYBRID: any hybrid produced in the wild or in cultivation that is not engineered by man

NODE: a joint on a stem or pseudobulb that usually bears a whorl of leaves, a bract or a single leaf.

PELORIC: of or relating to abnormal growth by one or more flower parts of a duplicate part

PISTIL: the female, seed-producing organ of the flower, which consists of the ovary, stigma and sometimes style

PSEUDOBULB: the thickened portion of an orchid plant that looks like a bulb and stores water for the plant; very common among epiphytic orchids, and vital to sympodial orchids

RHIZOME: a stem bearing its own roots; it lies on or just under the surface of the growing medium and progressively sends up leafy shoots from its tip or apex

SEMIALBA: coloration of a white flower with a colored lip

SEPAL: one of the outer three parts of an orchid flower

SLC.: refers to the fact that this genus is a combination of *Sophronitis*, *Laelia* and *Cattleya*

SPECIMEN ORCHID: a large, well-grown plant that is such a fine example of its kind that it exemplifies the group

SPHAGNUM: moss, particularly New Zealand sphagnum, used as a potting material because it retains moisture

STAMEN: the male organ of a plant that bears the pollen

STIGMA: the part of the pistil that receives the pollen, resulting in fertilization.

SUBSTANCE: durability and heavy structure, in reference to an orchid flower

SYMPODIAL: having new shoots arise from rhizomes of previous growth

TERETE: cylindrical, the shape of many orchids' leaves

TERRESTRIAL: growing in soil (or in the layer of humus on top of the soil)

TETRAPLOID: having four sets of chromosomes, which in orchids generally leads to superior (though fewer) flowers that are slower to mature

TREE FERN: a popular potting medium for orchids, derived from tropical/subtropical fern, that can be shredded for use in containers or in slab form for mounting orchids

UMBELLATE: bearing a strong resemblance to an umbrella

UNIFOLIATE: having one leaf per pseudobulb

VINICOLOR: wine red in color

ORCHIDS FOR ENTHUSIASTS

When you become more involved in growing orchids, you will undoubtedly send for new catalogues, attend orchid society meetings, discuss your acquisitions with fellow orchid growers and look forward to adding to your collection. However, while you may have mastered growing Cattleyas, Paphiopedilums and Phalaenopsis, other varieties offered for sale may not be all that familiar to you. You might, for example, admire an *Angraceum leonis* one day. "It looks wonderful," you may think, "but can I grow it?" What sort of conditions does it need? You can ask the purveyor of orchids you buy for advice in caring for them and you can look here where, at a glance, you'll most likely learn what basic culture your wished-for plant requires.

Forty orchids are featured in the Orchid Portraits. Here are additional orchids, by genus, that can be grown under lights, on a windowsill or in a greenhouse, but which are listed here separately as they are somewhat more demanding or more challenging to obtain. To simplify the growing instructions for unfamiliar varieties of orchids you wish to try, I have condensed the most significant needs of the most popular varieties. I have also indicated their ease of flowering, although you must bear in mind that this is not an exact science and what blooms easily for some is more difficult for others.

GENUS	TEMPERATURE	LIGHT	FLOWERING	HINTS
Aerides	W to I	◑	Slightly Difficult to Difficult	Pot in a loose mix. Best in a basket. They don't like to be repotted; disturb their roots only when necessary
Angraceum	I to C	○ to ◑	Easy	Small varieties good for growing under lights. Repot only every 3 or 4 years.
Ascocenda	W	○	Easy to Slightly Difficult	Likes high humidity. Best grown in slatted baskets. When plant has outgrown its basket, set in a larger basket without removing from smaller basket.

Cattleya aclandiae *is a wonderful orchid species that has been used extensively in hybridizing.*

If someone who knew nothing about orchids were asked what the common name of these orchids were, in all probability he would answer "spider orchids." And he'd be right. These small, lithe flowers are delicate, but when appearing en masse on a flowering plant with numerous inflorescences, they put on quite a display, as seen in this Brassia Rex 'Monterey.'

Genus	Temperature	Light	Flowering	Hints
Aspasia	I	◐	Easy	Pot plant tightly in the mix. Give lots of water when in growth. Don't ever allow them to dry out completely.
Bifrenaria	I to W	◐	Easy	Good windowsill plants. Repot only every 2 or 3 years. Decrease watering for about 3 to 5 weeks after flowering.
Brassia	I	◐	Easy	Good for beginners. Many Brassias are fragrant. Protect from midday sun.
Catasetum	I	◐	Easy to Slightly Difficult	When new growth appears give them warm, moist atmosphere. After active growth stops, give plants a rest period with less water and cooler temperatures.
Cattleya	I to W	○	Easy	Needs good drainage. Miniature Cattleyas are great for windowsills.
Cirrhopetalum	I	◐	Easy to Difficult	Grow on tree fern slabs or in small pots. Great for growing under lights.
Cymbidiums	C to W	◐	Easy to Slightly Difficult	Fertilize heavily from January through July. Summer outdoors. Let remain until temperatures drop to low 40s to high 30s to initiate bud formation. Plant in pots with large bark chunks. High light needed during summer and early fall.

Genus	Temperature	Light	Flowering	Hints
Dendrobium	C, I, W	○ to ◐	Easy to Difficult	Provide good drainage. Underpot so roots don't rot. Check to see where your Dendrobium comes from geographically and provide the same culture.
Epidendrum	I	◐	Easy	Good beginner plant. Use fir bark or tree fern as potting medium. If plants have firm pseudobulbs, give high light; if soft leaved, give diffuse light.
Laelia	I	○ to ◐	Easy to Difficult	Let Laelia rest after flowering. Dry out thoroughly between waterings. Pot in fir bark or tree fern. Small varieties are good for growing under lights and on windowsills.
Masdevallia	C to I	◐	Easy to Difficult	Use small pots. Provide very good drainage.
Maxillaria	C to I	◐	Easy	Give high humidity and a shaded location in summer. Give a short rest period. Pot in osmunda and sphagnum moss.
Miltonia, Brazilian	I to W	◐	Easy	Provide good drainage. Don't pack the potting mix too tightly as the roots need good air circulation. Give high humidity and partial shade.
Miltonia, Colombian	C to I	◐	Easy to Slightly Difficult	To induce good flowering, keep pot-bound. Plants like high humidity.

This orchid, Epidendrum longipetalum, *never fails to attract attention and is a relatively easy orchid for the beginner to succeed with.*

Here's an example of a very floriferous yellow Dendrobium. Notice that there are many buds still remaining on the plant. Therefore, even after the flowers on the plant die, new ones will open, keeping this plant in bloom for months at a time.

A spectacular Brazilian species, Laelia purpurata *comes in numerous colors. Shown here is one of the most beautiful,* Laelia purpurata *var.* corulea.

Here's a close-up of a typical *Oncidium* flower. Note the large yellow lip and, without stretching the imagination too far, the appearance of a lady in a full shirt dancing. This is how *Oncidiums* got the common name "dancing ladies."

This very striking *Paphiopedilum Magic Lantern* is a must for lovers of pink-flowered orchids. If you can get this orchid, a relatively new hybrid, don't hesitate to add it to your collection.

GENUS	TEMPERATURE	LIGHT	FLOWERING	HINTS
Odontoglossum	I to C	◑	Easy to Slightly Difficult	Grow in a small pot in an epiphytic mix. Good for growing under lights and on windowsills.
Oncidium	W, I, C	○	Easy to Slightly Difficult	Provide good humidity and light. Give a rest period after flowering.
Paphiopedilum	I to W	◑	Easy	Keep constantly moist.
Phalaenopsis	I to W	◑	Easy	Provide a semi-shaded spot. Don't let mix dry out.
Phragmipedium	I	○ to ◑	Easy to Slightly Difficult	These terrestrial orchids like to be kept constantly wet.
Pleurothallis	C, I, W	◑	Easy to Difficult	Pot in a mixture including New Zealand sphagnum moss to help retain moisture. They need high humidity. Grow in semi-shade. Repot as seldom as possible.

Yet another trend in Phalaenopsis breeding is toward smaller, more branching plants with beautiful colors. Phalaenopsis Be Tris 'Cutie' provides small clusters of white flowers with a brightly colored and dark lip.

Vanda Adrienne provides raspberry- and rose-colored, large flowers for those who can grow these wonderful orchids.

GENUS	TEMPERATURE	LIGHT	FLOWERING	HINTS
Renanthera	W	○ to ◑	Slightly Difficult	Grow in clay pots or baskets in a somewhat coarse mix. Plants like high humidity.
Sophronitis	C to I	◑ to ○	Easy to Slightly Difficult	Can be grown successfully in a pot, but some growers prefer mounting them on a tree fern slab and misting them often.
Stanhopea	I	◑	Slightly Difficult	Grow in baskets or on tree fern slabs, as the flowers grow on pendulous spikes. Keep evenly moist; provide high humidity and good air circulation.
Trichopilia	I	◑ to ○	Easy	Bright light but not direct sun. Require absolutely perfect drainage for the roots to stay healthy. Put some osmunda under broken pieces of crockery at the bottom of the pot.
Vanda	W	○	Slightly Difficult to Difficult	Need 6 full hours of sun each day to bloom. Plants grow very tall. Very high humidity required. Not orchids for the beginner.
Zygopetalum	I to C	◑ to ○	Easy	Wonderful aroma. They need good air circulation when the humidity is high. Don't mist these orchids. Provide good drainage.

SOURCES OF ORCHID PLANTS AND SUPPLIES

Most of the orchid growers listed below will provide you with a free listing or catalogue of their offerings. There may be a small fee for some of the catalogues. These suppliers are just a sampling of the many orchid sources of which you can avail yourself. A wide variety of orchids are sold at local orchid society sales tables.

You may find yourself offering members of your orchid society divisions of your plants and vice versa. One of the most exciting events for orchid growers are local orchid society auctions, where you can find wonderful and unusual orchids at excellent prices.

Joining the American Orchid Society (AOS) will provide you with a constant source of orchid growers, plus an incredible amount of information. In addition to receiving a monthly magazine, members of the AOS receive a 10% discount on books and other orchid literature available from its extensive orchid book list. For further information and a membership application, write to: The American Orchid Society, 6000 S. Olive Avenue, West Palm Beach, Florida 33405 or call (407) 585-8666.

ORCHID GROWERS

ADAGENT ACRES
2245 Floral Way
Santa Rosa, CA 95403-2414
(707)575-4459

ANGRACEUM HOUSE, THE
10385 East Drive
Grass Valley, CA 95945
(916) 273-9426

CARTER AND HOLMES
No. 1 Mendenhall Road
P.O. Box 668
Newberry, SC 29108
(803) 276-0579

ELMORE ORCHIDS
324 Watt Road
Knoxville, TN 37922
(615) 966-5294

FORDYCE ORCHIDS,
ORINDA and TONKINS
* ORCHIDS*
1330 Isabel Avenue
Livermore, CA 94550
(510) 447-7171

GEORGE SHORTER
* ORCHIDS*
P.O. Box 16952
Mobile, AL 36616
(205) 443-7469

GOLD COUNTRY ORCHIDS
390 Big Ben Road
Lincoln, CA 95648
(916) 645-8600

H & R NURSERIES
41-240 Hihimano Street
Waimanalo, HI 96795
(808) 259-9626

J & L ORCHIDS
20 Sherwood Road
Easton, CT 06612
(203) 261-3772

JEM ORCHIDS
6595 Morikami Park Road
Delray Beach, FL 33446
(407) 498-4308

KENSINGTON ORCHIDS
3301 Plyers Mill Road
Kensington, MD 20895
(301) 933-0036

KRULL-SMITH ORCHIDS
2815 Ponkan Road
Apopka, FL 32712
(407) 886-0915

LENETTE GREENHOUSES
1440 Pom Orchid Lane
Kannapolis, NC 28081
(704) 938-2042

MARILYN MIRRO ORCHIDS
1437 Pine Drive
Bayshore, NY 11706
(516) 666-3330

OAK HILL GARDENS
37W550 Binnie Rd.
W. Dundee, IL 60118
(708) 428-8500

ORCHID ART
1433 Kew Avenue
Hewlett, NY 11557
(516) 374-6426

ORCHID WORLD INTERNA-
    TIONAL, INC.
10885 S.W. 95th Street
Miami, FL 33176
(800) 367-6720

ORCHIDS BY HAUSERMANN,
    INC.
2N134 Addison Road
Villa Park, IL 60181-1191
(708) 543-6855

OWENS ORCHIDS
P.O. Box 365
Pisgah Forest, NC 28768
(704) 877-3313

PALESTINE ORCHIDS
Route 1, Box 312
Palestine, WV 26160
(304) 275-4781

RF ORCHIDS, INC.
28100 S.W. 182nd Avenue
Homestead, FL 33030
(305) 245-4570

RICHELLA ORCHIDS
2881 Booth Road
Honolulu, HI 96813
(808) 538-6637

ROD MCLELLAN CO., The
1450 El Camino Real
S. San Francisco, CA 94080
(415) 871-5655

SIAM ORCHIDS
4506 Kiowa
Pasadena, TX 77504
(713) 487-5670

STEWART ORCHIDS
3376 Foothill Road
Carpinteria, CA 03013
(805) 684-5448

SUNSWEPT ORCHID
    LABORATORIES
3860 Sunswept Drive
Studio City, CA 91604
(818) 506-7271

TROPICAL ORCHID FARM
P.O. Box H
Haiku, HI 96708
(808) 572-8569

WORLD OF ORCHIDS, A
2501 N. Old Lake Willison
    Road
Kissimmee, FL 34747
(407) 396-1887

ZUMA CANYON ORCHIDS,
    INC.
5949 Bonsall Drive
Malibu, CA 90265
(310) 457-9771

SOURCES OF ORCHID SUPPLIES

DYNA GROW CORPORATION
1065 Broadway
San Pablo, CA 94806
(800) 365-GROW

HYDROFARM
3135 Kerner Blvd.
San Rafael, CA 94901
(800) 634-9999

HYDROFARM EAST
208 Route 13
Bristol, PA 19007
(800) 227-4567

INDOOR GARDENING
    SUPPLIES
P.O. Box 40567-AO
Detroit, MI 45240
(313) 426-9080

OFE INTERNATIONAL, INC.
12100 S.W. 129th Court
Miami, FL. 33186
(305)253-7080

TROPICAL PLANT PROD-
    UCTS, INC.
P.O. Box 547764
Orlando, FL 32854
(407) 293-2451

Index